ORLANDO'S SLEEP

An Autobiography of Gender
by Jennifer Spry

New Victoria Publishers

Published by New Victoria Publishers Inc., a feminist, literary, and cultural organization, PO Box 27, Norwich, VT 05055-0027.

Printed and Bound in USA
1 2   3   4   5   2002   2000   1999   1998   1997

Library of Congress Cataloging-in-Publication Data
Spry, Jennifer, 1946-
    Orlando's Sleep: an autobiography of gender/by Jennifer Spry.
    p.   cm.
    ISBN 0-934678-80-4
    1. Spry, Jennifer, 1946- . 2. Transsexuals--Australia-
    -Biography.   3. Lesbians--Australia--Biography.
    4. Transsexualism.   5. Lesbianism.   I. Title.
    HQ77. 8. S695A3   1997
    305.9'066---dc21   96-45119
                                                  CIP

This book is dedicated to Sam

The goal of life is living in agreement with nature.
Zeno 335–263 B.C.

Acknowledgments

Many people have come and gone from my life over the years, especially the last five, as I went through my transition from that person who was John, to that same person who is now Jennifer. As in all lives, and books about lives, there is insufficient room in this section to mention, let alone thank, everyone who deserves my thanks. There are some people, though, against whom it would be a serious slight if they were not thanked individually.

There are two people in particular who deserve more thanks than I can ever give them. The first is my son, Sam, who has stood by me at all times over the last few years, and defended me on more occasions than I know of. The second is Laurie, someone else who has stood firmly by me and ended up a best friend, even after everything we went through together.

Two others are Betty Dixon, who guided me through many a crisis and kept me securely grounded, even when I doubted my own ability and sanity, and my partner Michelle Proctor who has had the courage, and given her time, to help with this book. It is usually seen as a cliché to say "without a particular person this book would not have been possible" but in this case it is true about both these wonderful women.

I do wish, as well, to specifically thank Lisa Nativi, Marje Stewart, Pat Starr, William Sloane-Coffin, Ina Anderson, Beth Dingman, Fred and Marje Thomas, Ferne Chase, Pat Owen, Deb Fisk, Kevin Moriarty, Pam Harrison, Alexis Teitz-Gersumky, and Nina Landis for her photos.

I also offer my thanks to all those people whose lives have touched mine over the years and seen in me a person and friend, rather than someone to fear, and consequently have not turned away.

And to those who have turned away, the loss is theirs.

Some names and incidents in this book have been changed; I regret that the intolerance of our society makes this deceit necessary.

Jennifer Spry, 1996

Contents

Introduction

Why, now that I am a butterfly
do I talk of caterpillars?
Why, now that I am a swan
do I talk of ugly ducklings?

I talk of these things
so that you
may learn my history,
and perhaps save others
from having to live it.

When I visited Australia in June 1993 my cousin asked, "If you don't want to make love to a man why did you go to all the trouble of having a sex change operation?" I felt my stomach sink with a rush. After six months of detailed letters going between us on the subject of my gender dysphoria I couldn't believe she had asked the question.

Some transgendered people, too, have looked at me askance and said, "Are you crazy, after all these years I'm just dying to meet a man and have him bonk me stupid. What's the point of having a vagina if not for sex with a man?" Even some lesbians allude to the question when they look at me and cognitively see only a man who has had his penis removed and think that *he* is living on a diet of hormones and delusions.

I think the confusion arises because the word 'sex' (as used to define the categories 'man' and 'woman') has become conflated and confused in people's minds with the word 'sexuality' (used to define categories such as gay, bisexual, heterosexual,

1

etc.). This results in people thinking, as my cousin thought, that my having a sex change operation meant that I was changing my *sexuality* –that after the operation I would automatically want to have intercourse with men—even though in the past I had always 'slept' with a woman. This is not the case; I have not changed my preference for a partner, I am now Lesbian Transgendered or Transgendered Lesbian.

To use the word gender, however, indicates a state of being; a state of being male, female, or maybe even some other option. Also, feminists have, for a long time, been using the word gender in preference to the word sex to show that social and cultural values determine the way society defines behaviors associated with our birth-assigned sex. With this in mind I prefer the use of the term gender (transgender) to the term sex (transsexual) because it has less preconceived and socially negative definitions applied to it—it also avoids the confusion that occurs between the words sex and sexuality. It is not my sexuality that was crossed, but my gender. (Perhaps the use of the word, transsexual, could be more accurately applied these days to those people who have moved from being heterosexual to gay, or from lesbian to bisexual, those who have crossed—trans—from one socially perceived sexuality to another.)

What needs to be recognized as well is, once people who are transgendered have sorted out their lives and are living in their true gender, then their choice of partner, or partners, changes the terminology needed to describe their sexuality, despite the fact that their sexuality has remained the same (unless they were and remain bisexual). For example, where once I was seen by society as a heterosexual male, I am now seen as a lesbian.

Added to all this is the confusion that results from our patriarchal society equating 'normal' with heterosexual. Since I was having an operation to make myself 'normal' in my eyes, then in the eyes of society, a part of that achieved 'normality' would be the desire to have intercourse with men, since according to society that's what 'normal' women do.

Wrong, or in the language of my fourteen-year-old son, NOT!

2

I have not changed my preference for a partner, I am now a Transgendered Lesbian.

In fact I don't believe I have psychologically changed much at all, despite all the physical changes. I have just shifted physically from being associated with one group that society calls men toward the other it calls women. No one asked my opinion the day I was born. The doctor just looked at a minuscule piece of flesh between my legs, and told my parents to dress me in blue. In 1946 he didn't even know he could *make* a mistake in picking between pink and blue. In truth I have probably ended up somewhere between the two 'acceptable' average points (as I have always been) but now I live on the other side of the divide and am perceived as more woman than man.

As far as I am concerned I have had to make my own choices, divorced from the existing patriarchal rules. I have never been sexually interested in men. As a teenager I wanted sexual contact with women, I married a woman, and now I want to live with a woman. Despite my physical appearance at birth, I am, and believe I always have been, female gendered and sexually lesbian.

'A man wearing women's clothes' is the most common way people imagine a transgendered person. In some cases, when a person cannot easily 'pass,' this may be the visual impression given. It makes that person conspicuous and often invokes fear or disgust from those they meet.

Quite often transgendered people are also confused with transvestites or cross-dressers. It is my understanding that these two groups wear women's clothes to achieve some degree of sexual satisfaction. It is the wearing of the clothes that is important to transvestites and cross-dressers and at no time do they seriously consider giving up their gender. For a transgendered person the situation is very different. The desire to dress as a woman is only a small facet of their whole being. It is only the outward sign of the inner turmoil.

This inner turmoil expresses its presence in transgendered people in many ways and to many different degrees. It is not possible to point to one person's actions or experiences and claim

3

they are definitive of or diagnostic for all transgendered people. Some people show no outward signs of their inner torment until they finally make the decision to change over and live in their gender of preference. Others will, fairly early on in life, move into the world of sex work and nightclub performance. Some begin living in their preferred gender as early as possible. One woman I know of (male-to-female transgendered) started when she was about twelve by stealing her mother's birth-control pills. The method I chose was to remain at home and 'in the closet,' cross-dressing as often as possible.

A pioneer in gender studies, John Money, wrote that we all have a Core Anatomic Identity, an identity that he hypothesized is formed before birth. He said it is this 'identity' that lets children know at an early age that they are either 'little girls' or 'little boys.' It is what, I believe, told me at the age of five, despite all the physical evidence to the contrary, that I was a girl.

I didn't know what sex was. I didn't know what a lesbian was. I doubt I even knew that society's measure of whether a child is a boy or a girl is made by the presence or absence of a penis. And it was because of the presence of that minuscule piece of flesh that I was labeled a boy. I knew, however, I was not a boy, I was a girl.

The way I expressed my transgenderism (gender dysphoria) was by wearing, as often as possible, the clothes that our society traditionally associates with women. This was probably because, when I was young, it was the easiest method of self expression available to me. My wearing of those items of clothing normally associated by society with being female gave me periods of time when I could deceive myself into a private world where I was accepted as female. This is not a method of expression or escape used by all who are transgendered because, as with everything, we all chose a different route, but it was the method I used and it became a major part of my existence. I did not consider my wearing of women's clothes as cross-dressing; it was when I was dressed as a man that I felt cross-dressed.

Over the years my need to be seen, and accepted, as a girl or woman grew to be an obsession, but I resisted it for the sake of my family and friends, as well as for my own position in society. Eventually, I reached the point where I had to stop living as other people wanted me to live and start living for myself; to become the person I knew myself to be.

If you find all this confusing, imagine how difficult it is explaining it to people who have no knowledge of or interest in transgenderism and would in most cases prefer that it had never touched their lives. I have sometimes even wondered if it's worth trying to get people to understand. Perhaps it would be better if I just wandered off, to be remembered as 'the eccentric son who thought he was a woman,' to go like my great-uncle 'Black Jack' did and live apart from the family, to be talked of only in hushed tones until time dissolves me from their memories. If I did this though no one would learn from my experiences. I would die a forgotten enigma.

To not write also seems to me the same as remaining closeted, and perhaps condemning others to remain so too. I feel committed to at least trying to show that I, and others like me, are not strange, perverted creatures to be shunned and reviled.

There are not many of us. Some estimates from American studies say as few as one child in every hundred thousand is born transgendered and that perhaps twenty percent of those are lesbian or gay. The majority of transgendered people, perhaps ten percent, who get as far as having surgery, just want to immerse themselves in their chosen gender and disappear. Very few of us have the drive or ability to put our stories down on paper; so I feel I should.

Eminent writers such as Jan Morris have also tackled this subject, as have scientific writers such as Richard Green and John Money; and heterosexual transgendered people such as Caroline Cossey and Katherine Cummings. Recently an excellent book was published by Kate Bornstein looking at the political aspects of a lesbian transgendered lifestyle. All of these people tackle the subject from a different perspective and all are worth reading.

I started writing this book in 1991 in America, sitting at my computer looking south, toward Australia, through the windows of a converted New England school house in Strafford, Vermont. The school house was built in the early 1800s and throughout its years I am sure it had seen many fine scholars come and go. I sometimes wondered which teacher or pupil was looking over my shoulder as I wrote.

I was renting it for the winter of 1990. It was a beautiful retreat. Its multi-paned front window overlooked open fields and a stone-walled country road, arched over by large, old maple trees. Beyond the walls were the old farm fields, green and lush with meadow-grass and wild flowers in summer. In January they were buried deep in a smoothing cover of thick, white snow that sparkled like a sequined shawl in the sub-zero winter air. Behind me I could hear the brook, gurgling along under a layer of ice, as it tumbled toward and over the Old City Falls.

It was like a doll house and suited my feeling that I was just entering a late-life puberty. That it had been selected as the site for my coming out seemed more than coincidence and I had no problem believing in providence as I sat there typing.

Because of my own situation, the main emphasis of this book will be on those people who change from outwardly male to outwardly female. Many people go the other way, from outwardly female to male, but I can only speak of my own experience.

Much of what I write is tragic as this is a subject that can and does destroy families; it can lead to the alienation of both the transgendered people and their family from society, sometimes even to suicide. Some pages of this autobiography tend to sound highly emotional, and at the time they were written that was how I felt. I hope that the words I used convey the intensity of feeling that all this invoked in me. Also, through my reading on the subject and from discussions I have had with others, I know that the incidents I write about have happened to most transgendered people in one way or another.

I have found, too, that there are many similarities between coming-out as transgendered and coming-out as lesbian or gay. Many of the same barriers exist and many of our battles can be very similar. Until my late teens my life was probably no harder

6

than that of many other lesbians, I just fought different battles as I struggled to find my own identity and come to terms with it. As with many lesbians (and gay men) I eventually succumbed as a teenager and retreated to the closet.

During my coming-out period, which started in the late 1980s and continues even now in various ways, I have received strength and affirmation from reading the stories of lesbians who have had to confront families and friends who held similar beliefs to those held by my family. Without the courage of these women who preceded me in putting their stories into print, my own change-over would have been immeasurably harder as there were no comparable transgender stories that I could find at the time.

The main difference in the lesbian coming-out stories I read, compared to my own experience, was one of degree: I wanted more than the right to live with a same-sex partner; I wanted the right to change my apparent gender *and* live with a same-sex partner.

There is also a lighter side to some of the events I write about. I needed to look for and find this humor in order to retain a balanced perspective in all that was happening during the physical changes I made. (I hope readers of this book will also be able to find irony and humor in its pages.) One also needs to maintain a sense of the ridiculous and have the ability to occasionally laugh as *faux-pas* are committed and lessons learned. A perspective must be maintained between the everyday happiness of living and the ever-present shadow of the confusion and isolation in a transgendered life.

Our society can be very intolerant of those who are deemed to be different, be it intellectually, racially or sexually, and we all develop various methods of coping with this intolerance. It is not because I am transgendered that I needed to write this book, it is because an intolerant society has a rule that says there can be only two genders, between which a person cannot move. Nor can they be somewhere in between. Society believes that I and others like me are breaking the rules and therefore require punishment.

It is my hope that this book will help show that the rules are ridiculous, based only on the fear and ignorance of the rule makers, and that the rules should be abandoned so that more understanding can be shown toward a small minority group.

Chapter One

My name is Jennifer and I was born in September 1946 in Melbourne, Australia. Jennifer is not the name I was given at birth but the one I chose many years later. I was the first born of a family that would eventually have three other daughters. Both my parents were loving and attentive as was my extended family of grandmothers, aunts and uncles. We had enough money to live first in a small flat and then, when controls on building were lifted after the war, for my parents to build a new family home. There was no discomfort or trauma that I can remember and my childhood was a time of happiness. It is from this firm base that I started to grow.

During my first four years, before my first sister was born, the main friend I played with on a regular basis was the only other child in our small block of flats, 'Lily-bell.' My memory is a bit vague but I remember a sand pit on the roof of the garage and, probably because they came with me into later years, various stuffed toys including a dog, a duck, and a cat that meowed when you pulled its ears.

My mother, June, stayed home and ran the house while my father, Edwin, worked in the city. My father's main contact with me in my pre-teenage years was driving me to school each morning and reading to me, usually from Christopher Robin books, before bed. My mother fulfilled all my other needs. This was also the normal parental pattern in the families of most of my friends and was certainly not unique to my own family.

As in many families, my maternal grandmother did much of the child care in my early years. She lived with her mother in

Camberwell. Both of them were widowed, although I have a vague memory of my great-grandfather who must have died when I was three or four. My grandmother used to recall her enjoyment in taking me in the pram to the local shopping strip because people would comment on "what a pretty child" I was.

When I was about eight or nine our next door neighbor said one day as we stood outside our house, "What beautiful hair you have. It is wasted on a boy. It should be on a girl." The comment struck me hard and I silently said to myself, "Oh but it is on a girl, it *is*. If only I could tell you." I am sure that the other people involved in these incidents forgot them in a moment, but for me they hit a chord that I can still hear.

These moments were particularly important to me because I was born transgendered; because by the time I was five I felt I was not as I appeared to the outside world. I kept this secret for many years. I should have asked for advice but I did not know how. Five year old boys do not go to their mother and say, "I want to be a girl," or rarely more than once anyway.

Even my basic human training was affected. My mother explained to me that little girls sit to urinate and little boys stand. From that day on, unless there was no alternative, I never stood in front of a toilet bowl. How old was I at the time? Maybe four or five at the most.

I remember one Christmas opening a small parcel and getting my first multi-bladed pocket knife. As I opened the various blades, screwdrivers and points I came to a nail file. I looked at it and said happily, "Oh good, I need a nail file." It hurt when the room full of adults laughed, and said, "Little boys don't need to file their nails." I know now that they were wrong, but that is immaterial.

I watched my mother and other women around me and tried to imitate them when I felt that no one was watching. I sat on the couch with my legs together, or walked with my hands bent at the wrist. Alone in my room I brushed my hair to as feminine a style as I could achieve, or covered it all with a handkerchief, draped like a scarf. These examples may seem trivial but when you know that, despite all outward appearances, you are a girl and you can't tell anyone, they are incredibly important.

I do not have any real memories from before I was five so I do not know if I showed any overt transgendered, or even homosexual, signs at a younger age. Those members of my family who remember me from then claim they do not remember any, but they weren't looking for signs anyway. They just thought I was a "pretty" boy.

The year before I started school was when my parents built their new house in the suburb of Toorak. It was an area that was becoming popular at the time. It was affluent, close to good shopping and public transport. In those quieter days it was a 15 minute drive from the business area of the city. It was a two story brick house and even though, because of post war rationing, there were still restrictions on the size of houses, it was still large enough for my first sister and me to each have our own room. The block was also large enough for my parents to add on extra rooms when my other sisters were born. The size of the house meant I always had my own room and therefore the privacy to explore my femininity as I grew.

I started primary school in 1952 at Melbourne Church of England Grammar School, a prestigious boys-only school. That year I was the youngest and smallest "boy" in the school and was given the honor of presenting a bouquet of flowers to the wife of the guest-of-honor at our annual prize-giving day. At the rehearsal I was shown how to hold the flowers, walk calmly onto the stage, pass them to outstretched arms, curtsy, turn, then walk calmly off. On prize day I stood in the wings of the stage, waiting nervously for my cue (a nudge by a teacher) then hurrying out toward the dais. There were over two hundred people in the hall and they all started to clap. I thrust the flowers toward the woman, curtsied quickly, then turned and hurried, almost ran, off the stage. My shy six-year-old heart was racing with fear and embarrassment.

The fact that I was taught to curtsy for the occasion, an act which is normally a female one, has only become important to

11

me with hindsight, but it is one more example of how that which would be normally insignificant, has made a lasting impression.

When I was about six we bought a vacation house in the town of Portsea, south of Melbourne on the Mornington Peninsula. It was an old double-fronted Victorian weather-board house with a full width verandah and panels of red, etched glass on either side of the front door. It had a central passage with two bedrooms on either side and mine was the one to the right as you came in. Again I had the privacy to explore my feelings and often fantasized about being a young girl or teenager at the beach.

We spent most of our vacations there, especially the summer ones, and at least every second weekend for the next ten years. The house grew in size over the years as we added a new kitchen and a bunk house. It was always an exciting place. It was in an undeveloped area with plenty of scope for exploring and swimming and lots of freedom. Bushfires were sometimes a threat and a summer never went by without at least one tiger-snake being seen, some up to two meters long. My mother even claimed that the house was haunted and that she had seen the form of a woman by the front door. This haunting was confirmed by a number of people who found that they could not sleep well in the front bedroom across from mine, and this added to the aura of the place for me.

Here I also learned the beauty of wildlife, birds in particular. I spent many hours watching them and found out how frustrating it was to try and photograph a small brown bird in a thick bush. I took roll after roll of black and white film only to end up with dozens of photos of tea-tree bushes with nothing but a slightly darkened area in the center where I insisted the bird was, or had been.

I enjoyed watching the birds' agile movements through the branches and their soaring freedom of the sky. A twist of feathers on an invisible air current animated and moved them with such lightness that they appeared like a heat shimmer, or a leaf on a breeze. I could watch them happily for hours, no matter how common or visually plain.

I also learned to appreciate the vivacity and courage of one bird in particular, the female Blue Wren. Many years later, I adopted her colloquial name—Jenny.

During those childhood years I roamed the adjoining bush either alone or with a friend. Later, when I was ten or eleven, I was allowed to walk or ride my bike the two kilometers or so into town. There was little risk involved in this in the 1950s but as children my sisters and I were never encouraged to roam too far from home. I rarely went against my parents wishes and was very nervous and shy if any of my friends suggested that we go off on any type of adventure. I sometimes went with my friends, and had lots of fun, but I was never entirely happy if I thought that what I was doing would not be approved of by my parents.

The punishment for disobedience, or any other sin, was never corporal. I and my sisters would get a stern talking to as my mother told us how disappointed she was in our behavior. For the really bad sins she resorted to saying, "Just wait until your father gets home," but nothing ever happened when he did. On one occasion, when I was about twelve a friend, Tim, and I found a newly dead rat. We convinced a little girl who lived nearby that it was, in fact, a kitten and was really only asleep. We gave it to her and told her to take it into her mother. When my mother found out, she became very quiet and looked at me, and said, "That was a very cruel thing to do. I just don't know what you were thinking of."

I spent the rest of the afternoon sulking around the house convinced that, for such a horrible crime, I would at least get a sound smacking with the jam spoon, or be sent to bed without dinner—both punishments that I knew were inflicted on my friends by their parents. When my father came home I was standing in the kitchen waiting. My mother related the story and he looked down at me. "I am terribly disappointed in you," he said. "That was a very cruel thing to do. I thought you would be more grown up and know not to do such a thing."

This form of 'punishment by shame' was not physically painful but it worked. Over the five minute lecture that seemed to go on for an hour, the sentences got longer and his voice got slower. Talk of disappointment and dissolution convinced me that I was beyond redemption. At the end he finished with, "Now, we won't talk about it any more. But if something like this ever happens again..." And there the subject was left hanging.

My father never got involved in giving permission, he would always answer a request with "go and ask your mother." Later, when we pressed him for permission for things that we knew he would not approve of, like staying out after midnight, he would give a sigh of desolation and say, "Well, you know my feelings on the matter, but if you really must." Normally this would be enough for me to cancel any plan I was making. If I persisted, and went against his wishes, his words would ensure that I did not enjoyed myself.

Although I gave plenty of signs of gender confusion to my parents during my pre-puberty and puberty years, nothing was ever said to me and I can only assume that they thought I was going through a phase I would grow out of.

It needs, however, to be emphasized again that this was all happening in the 1950s in Melbourne. Not only did people not know about transgenderism, they did not normally talk about sex in any way either. We had no books in the house on the subject, nor was there any sex education at school. No one told me of the changes my body would go through at puberty. My sex education was supplied in fragments, often erroneously, by my friends who either had older brothers or had access to medical books belonging to their fathers. By the age of sixteen I was regularly checking my eyesight, and carefully looking for the hairs that I knew would soon be growing from the palm of my hand, because I had heard that these would result from masturbation. This lack of sexual education was not an occurrence unique to my family. It was common to the time and place (and sadly, may still be in many places).

The lack of intervention in my sexual and gender development at the time, however, probably saved me from the trauma of aversion therapy, or some other form of psychiatric 'cure.' This knowledge has now softened my past anger against my parents for what I saw as their apparent lack of guidance. In Australia there was no professional help for transgenderism.

My upbringing, and the subsequent handling of my gender confusion, was based on the morals of the 1940s and 1950s. It was obviously different in the 1980s and 1990s, and I don't want to suggest that I suffered unfairly. I don't feel that anyone in those days could have foreseen, let alone changed, where I was going.

My family was very loving but had the standard outlook of the era. Boys were boys and girls were girls. Homosexuality and other sexual variations existed but were never part of our family. We were a standard post-war family that was very close but never spoke of subjects like sex or religion that were deemed socially 'taboo.'

I was twenty-five and on the other side of the world in New York City before I found out there was a word for the way I felt, and that I was not alone.

Chapter Two

The first time I remember feeling I was not wholly a boy was during my first skiing trip with my parents to Mt. Buffalo in the Victorian High Plains. We stayed at the Mt. Buffalo Chalet, a magnificent old building built in 1910 and the only hotel there. It was in the first week of September 1951, near my fifth birthday.

That morning my father had already gone downstairs to breakfast and my mother and I were about to follow. I waited for my mother in a small bedroom where there was a dark wood wardrobe and a small dressing table, in the style of 1910. She was in the bathroom down the hallway and I was alone, looking out the window to the slopes, sitting on the bed swinging my legs, trying to fill time until she returned. Suddenly I had the thought that I was a girl. I don't remember thinking of myself as belonging to one gender or the other before that time, but from then on I felt I was a girl.

At the age of five I could not have known that what I was thinking would be interpreted by adults as abnormal. In my childish naiveté I don't think I even knew that I was thinking differently from any other child my age. By the time I was ten, however, I was using whatever opportunities came to me, via subterfuge or otherwise, to live as a girl.

As a child it was at my maternal grandmother's that I had the opportunity to explore myself and to expand my experiences with my femininity. Her house was a brick villa that she had lived in since my grandfather had it built for them in the 1920s. It was on a busy suburban street but set back behind a formal English-style garden. There was a low box-hedge along the road and large trees. The lawn was thick buffalo-grass and up one side was the orange gravel drive to the front door. In the rear of the house was another garden with over-sized trees and bushes which provided lots of secret places.

My grandmother was a very lively, outgoing person and I loved visiting her. She always had treats for me and let me do things that I was not allowed to do at home. This was before the time of television and we would cuddle together in an arm-chair after dinner and listen to radio plays. One night the last line of a scary mystery story was "don't drink that milk, it's poisoned." From then on we would quote the line to each other, with much giggling, every time I had a glass of milk. She also spent endless hours playing with me, even allowing me to ride on the running board of her 1947 Buick as she came up the drive. My favorite pastime however was dressing up.

My grandmother never threw away a thing and the cup-boards in the spare bedrooms were full of an endless supply of dresses, hats and shoes of every variety from my mother's child-hood as well as dresses and lovely wide hats belonging to my grandmother. Most of the clothes were in the easy, soft-flowing style of the 1920s or the more formal suits and skirts of the 1940s. I liked the 1920s dresses, their shorter style sweeping the floor around my short legs or hitched up with a belt to give a more 'authentic' look. I completed the outfits with long bead necklaces and wide brimmed hats and became, for an afternoon, 'a gay young thing who went to balls and dinners with famous people' and was called "Madam" by my grandmother. Make-up was brought out on occasion but I do not remember using it very often. I had the run of the house and spent many hours as Jennifer (although I did not select this name until many years later).

Often I would be left to spend a night or weekend at my grandmother's while my parents were at a party or away. These were wonderful visits. After my parents left, 'Little Nan' would allow me to dress in all manner of finery and I would wander around the house partaking in 'tea parties' and other trips of imagination. She never said that what we were doing was wrong. We both just saw it as fun. I don't think it ever entered her mind that it was damaging, and I don't believe it was. There were plenty of more masculine pleasures I could have found in that rambling yard and the disused rooms, such as climbing trees or exploring the store room and the old wooden boxes marked 'fidgets' and 'gadgets' in the garage. Sometimes I did, but I was given a free choice, and I usually chose to play dress-up.

I recall the sadness on Little Nan's face and within me when one evening after a visit she and I were told by my mother that I was not to play 'dress-up' any more. During the weekend Little Nan had taken me to the local shops, small Victorian buildings all lined up along Burke Road, and bought me ice cream cones and comic books as she did every time I went to stay. She knew all the shop keepers and they all knew me.

Back at her house we shared 'spiders,' lemonade with ice cream in it, served in a long soda glass with a spoon. In the afternoon I asked her to let me play dress up and we went to the closets in the spare room where she had the old clothes and hats she used to wear to the horse races when she was younger.

That evening my parents came to collect me. They were having a drink in the 'smoke-room.' I was still dressed up and I came in feeling very pleased and pretty in a long, green satin dress, high heels and a wide-brimmed summer hat. I smiled and said "hello" to my parents from the doorway, looking for a comment about how nice I looked. My mother turned to me and said, "Go and change into your own clothes, we are leaving soon."

I didn't reply. I just walked out of the room to go and change. As I left I heard my mother say to Little Nan, "I don't want John dressing up anymore. He is getting too old for that game."

"But he enjoys it so much," my grandmother said.

"I don't care, he is too old for it," my mother replied. "I don't want you to let him dress like that anymore. Please, don't let him do it ever again."

The sound of flat determination in my mother's voice told me that she meant it. My father, as usual, didn't say a word. He just sat there in his tweed jacket with his whisky and water and nodded in agreement. I was about ten at the time.

From that time on there were numerous occasions when I allowed 'Jennifer' to be herself. This was usually when, for some reason, I was home alone and could select clothes from my mother's closet. There was the ever present risk of being caught. The house was two storied and the bedrooms looked out on the street. I would peek from behind the blind, edging it from the window just far enough to see out, until a car pulled up outside the house. Time was vital. I knew from experience when someone was due home: in half an hour if it was a trip to the local milk bar; at 3 pm. when my sister would come running down the hill from school; at 5 pm. if my mother had said she would be home in time to cook dinner. I watched the clock carefully and felt the fear that I had not returned everything to its proper place and the rush of adrenaline when I was caught or had a close call. I learned that what I enjoyed was not approved of by my parents. I did whatever was necessary to hide my true self from public scrutiny.

I cannot begin to estimate how many hours I consumed in my clandestine activities as I moved around the house, blinds drawn, carefully pulling on the brass handles of my mother's lingerie draw, reaching in, lifting out an item and then gently closing the draw to the same point where I had found it. Her built-in robes with the full length mirrors on the outside held dresses that I would lift out, one at a time, try on and return with infinite care before closing the door and returning everything to just as it had been before.

Even when not actively 'cross-dressing' the desire remained with me. My imagination would wander to the potential joys of living openly as a girl whenever triggered by a related thought or occurrence. A picture in a school book, or an article in a paper was often enough, as was time spent alone with my thoughts, such as when we were traveling on one of the family trips my mother planned and organized for us.

19

Being an adventurous person my mother organized many trips over the years and most of them were arranged so that we could all go as a family. She was interested in anthropology and Australian history, especially when it involved the 'outback.' She spent hours looking at maps and reading books while developing a holiday plan.

In 1959, I broke my arm just before the start of the school holidays, which meant our holiday plans had to be changed, so she decided we should do a driving holiday to Queensland. Her plans, however, did not include the normal routes on sealed highways, driving from scenic point to scenic point as most people do. Her plan was to see the real outback on roads normally only used by local farmers in utilities, four wheel drives and stock trucks.

We set out in our very sedate Humber Hawk sedan and drove to Mildura, and then turned northeast and followed the Darling River from where it joins the Murray River to the Queensland border, and then came back down the highway through Canberra and Albury to Melbourne. The year we did this trip the road along the Darling was no more than two sandy wheel tracks linking the various sheep stations with the small river towns. Petrol was only available every three hundred miles or so and we had to carry our own fuel, as well as drinking water and food.

There were no green blankets of grass in the paddocks, just tussocks and small stands of trees with leaves like conifers, to minimize water loss. Between the larger towns were all-weather roads made of course gravel, raised above the surrounding plains just enough to keep them relatively dry and passable on those rare occasions when it did rain. They were bone-shaking to drive on. Alongside the road there were wide shallow spoon-drains and it was in these that we drove most of the time. They were much smoother than the road and we could speed along with the dust rising behind us. The only time that we drove back up onto the road was at a fence line, every ten or fifteen miles. Here there was a cattle grid set in the bed of the road instead of a gate and we rattled over it and then back down into the spoon-drain. As we drove, the red 'bull-dust' rose in clouds from the wheels of the car and infiltrated into every corner of the car.

Mirages shimmered along the horizon and approaching cars or trucks appeared rippled and distorted ahead of us as they emerged from the mirage to eventually pass us trailing their own cloud of dust. Sheep lay in the shade of trees and emus paced alongside us before veering suddenly away on long legs, their feathers bouncing like short, gray tulle skirts.

Finding a camp site each night was easy. We just pulled far enough off the road to have a little privacy and put up our tent. We did not have to be far off the road as we normally only saw cars in and around the small towns. On the road it was not uncommon to go for two days without seeing anyone else.

As we drove I bird watched, played games and day-dreamed of how it would be to live in this area of the country. I remember fantasizing about growing up on one of these sheep stations and being treated as a girl. It would be so easy, I thought, as it was very isolated and I could do my schooling via the Royal Flying Doctor Service 'School of the Air'—no one need ever know!

After this trip my mother set her sights on most places in the outback of New South Wales, southern Queensland and eastern South Australia. They bought a gray Land Rover station wagon and fitted it out with shelving and extra water tanks and fuel tanks to make it safe to travel through the desert areas that she loved so much. When they headed out of Melbourne the Land Rover was loaded down with extra spare wheels on the roof rack and shovels and jacks strapped to the back between specially made holders for the jerry cans of fuel and water. When they came back it was caked red outside with mud, and thick inside with fine dust that blew out in a cloud every time you slammed the door. And my mother would have filled the car with every imaginable rock, branch or long-horn Hereford skull that had caught her imagination. Her skin was burnt brown and her gray hair hung in strands, dry and brittle from washing in bore water.

Over the years she and my father reached all the isolated and historically important points that they could, including all the opal mining areas of Queensland and South Australia. They drove down the Strezleckie and Birdsville tracks well before they were part of the established tourist routes of Australia.

My mother amassed a huge collection of books on outback Australia and the country she had driven through. Since she was also a voracious reader of novels and travel books in general, every room in our house had large floor to ceiling book cases to accommodate her passion. After those shelves were full she stacked the books in corners and under tables in her bedroom.

With her love of travel she went wherever she could, including overseas. The first time she did this was in 1956. My parents, my sister and I flew from Sydney to Rome on a Qantas Super Constellation. The trip took three days including overnight stops in Darwin and Singapore. I was told that the airline was not allowed to fly over water at night.

When we arrived in Rome we hired a small Fiat 500, a car somewhat smaller than a Morris Mini, and with only about half the power. In this the four of us drove to Paris and then back along the French Riviera to Positano, south of Naples. We didn't have much money for the trip but my mother still had to see inside all the romantic palaces. In Paris she wanted to eat at Maxim's so we all went in and she ordered the cheapest meal she could. We each had an omelet. In Monte Carlo she put on her best dress and she and my father went in and had one bet each on the Roulette wheel.

We returned, after touring Italy and southern France, on the Orient Line ship *Orcades* from Naples to Melbourne via the Suez Canal. For me the highlight of the trip back was seeing flying fish and collecting the small plated-metal arrows that came with the red cherry in martinis. My sister and I insisted that our parents have at least one martini each night before dinner.

During these early years my femininity also expressed itself in my attitudes, choice of friends and pursuits. I was happiest when I could be with just one friend at a time. I did not like to be with large groups, even at parties.

I played traditional boys games with most of my friends, but I had one special friend. Around the age of ten or eleven, before I had my first pair of long pants, he used to come over after school and we would play 'dress-makers.' The basement of our house was a converted garage that was fitted out with some old furniture, cupboards and our toys, including a trunk full of old clothes that were used for dressing up. With the aid of this dress-up box and an old Singer pedal sewing machine my friend and I spent afternoons pretending to make clothes. We both wore dresses from the dress-up box and ran others through the needle-less sewing machine before delivering them to make-believe customers.

I don't remember feelings of fear or guilt while we played the game, or of being seen as we ran around the back yard in our dresses. It was a game that gave me a special kind of pleasure and I had a relationship with my friend that was different than what I had with my other friends. I felt a mutual understanding with him. I could be someone different than the self I shared with my other friends.

Then, when I was twelve, I had a remarkable experience. I can date it accurately because I had just recently been given a new bedroom and my chest of draws had a three-piece mirror on top of it. I was standing in front of the mirror getting dressed in my navy-blue school uniform when I was struck with the irrefutable knowledge that I was definitely a girl. I looked in the mirror and it was no longer a case of being confused, or just feeling like a girl, I knew I was one. The feeling that I had had since I was five suddenly solidified and from then on I knew, without a doubt, I was a girl. I stood there looking at myself in my blue shirt and tie and knew it was true, I wanted it to be. What until

23

then had been a sensing, now became a reality. I didn't think "how awful" or "how can I change this," I felt content.

With the benefit of hindsight I realize now that before that moment I had never deeply considered what being a girl or a boy meant. I had my own knowing, and I understood what it meant for me to know I was a girl, despite being told by society that I was a boy.

I think this realization provided me with some sort of subconscious support for what was to come. Ironically it was also the point from which all my sexual and gender confusions emanated and grew. From that morning on I was never totally certain how to accommodate my male body with my female mind, so I swung back and forth like a pendulum trying hard to be male, yet wanting to express my femininity. I ended up feeling paranoid that someone would see my feminine side, yet in my head I knew I was a girl and wanted the world to see and accept me as one. There was no one I could go to for help in solving my conundrum.

Around this time I also began regularly raiding my mother's and sisters' closets. I used their clothes, dolls, and on the rarest of occasions their make-up. Usually I tried to limit my visits to when there was no one else in the house. I stayed away from make up because it was so hard to get off, and again I was so self-conscious that I was sure my lips would still be red, even after vigorous rubbing with soapy water.

It was always hard to find a time when I felt sure that I would not get caught and I often made an error of judgment that resulted in awkward questions. These questions always came from my mother and were never followed up with any discussion or condemnation. The normal scenario was for her to come upon me unawares, and then, without saying a word, just turn and walk away, leaving me feeling bad but unsure why. After such a confrontation I would stop cross-dressing for some months, though rarely longer. Then one day 'Jennifer' would return and I would start all over again.

Cross-dressing became a regular habit over the rest of my

teen years. I took every opportunity I could. One night before my parents went out I took my mother's stockings and suspender belt. I couldn't wait until they'd left and locked myself in the bathroom and put them on. I sat on the toilet, put my leg up on the wash basin, carefully smoothed on the stockings and clipped them onto the suspender belt. I forgot that the window beside me was in direct view of my mother's bedroom. She was watching me. I put my long school pants on over the stockings and came out feeling very pretty.

My mother came around from her room and said, "Are you wearing stockings?"

I looked at her and said, "No, of course not. Why?"

She just said, "Okay," and went off to her party.

Nothing more was said. Over the years there were many times when she found me either wearing some item of her clothing or hiding something belonging to her or one of my sisters in my room. She never confronted me, talked to me, or tried to find out what I was doing, or why.

One day I arranged things so that I could stay home alone while the family drove 100 kilometers to our beach house. My excuse for not going was a rowing regatta at school. I had no intention of going to a rowing regatta; I was staying home to dress-up, and I knew I had from 9 a.m. until exactly 6 p.m. before they returned.

After they drove off I pulled down the blinds and stripped. Then I went to my mother's room and got out her clothes. The day was wonderful. I put on stockings, underwear, make-up and cotton and silk dresses. I went through every drawer and cupboard and tried on anything I liked. When I found an outfit I wandered around the house in it, wearing her shoes, and sat in chairs and savored the feeling of being 'truly female.'

This went on all day until, by late afternoon, I was wearing a back-zippered evening dress, and pretending that I had gone to a wonderful ball at which I danced the night away. I swirled through the house, curtsied to mirrors and danced around the living room, my arms held out to an invisible partner.

I completely lost track of time until, at exactly 6 p.m., I heard a car pull into the drive. My family was home. Clothes were strewn across my mother's bed, and I was wearing make-up and a grey evening-dress with layered petticoats.

I panicked, grabbed her clothes and threw them into the bottom of a closet and closed the door. As I struggled to get out of a full length evening-dress, my mother came up the stairs. I retreated to the toilet, rustling in layers of tulle and satin, and locked the door.

My mother called for me as she came through the house and eventually arrived outside my toilet refuge. I answered her from behind the locked door, naked, with the huge evening dress now piled up on the floor beside me.

"Why are you locked in the toilet?" she asked.

"Because I don't have any clothes on."

"Come out," she demanded"

"No," I replied, my voice quavering.

She then asked in a bemused tone, "Why don't you have any clothes on?"

"Because I've been weighing myself," I lied.

"Stop being so silly and come out," she demanded again.

"No," I replied, but less forcefully.

And so the confrontation continued with me becoming more scared, yet no less resolute, and my mother becoming more frustrated. Finally she went away and I was left alone.

With my heart pounding I raced out, stuffed the dress back in the closet with the others and closed the door with a shove. I hadn't even hung her clothes up.

I then ran naked to my room, praying that no one saw me, dressed in my own clothes, wiped the make-up off my face and, feeling guilty as hell, casually appeared in the kitchen.

Nothing was said about the incident. I waited all night, sure that one of my parents would come to talk to me about it but, as with every other time I was caught, both before and after, they didn't.

It was after occasions such as this that I swore I would never cross-dress again; yet my resolve always faded and I soon returned to my inner need for outward feminine expression.

I don't know what my mother thought or felt about all this because she never spoke to me about it. On one morning she came into my room as I was getting dressed and I saw her cry as she left me standing in a pair of her underpants. But still nothing was said. It must have been very hard for her. She had to carry all this on her own. I'm not sure my father knew. He says now that he didn't, but I wonder if it is possible for a married couple not to discuss what their children are doing, especially when it is potentially as devastating as transgenderism.

I assume that my mother had decided to wait and see what happened to me. To see if I grew out of it. In fact, all that happened as I got older was that I got better at hiding things. Considering the total lack of information on transgenderism she must have assumed that I was homosexual.

Although homosexuality was rarely spoken about she had some contact with the local florist and a milliner who were both homosexual. In those days homosexuality was a heavier stigma than it is now, so she must have been very worried about me. Not only would such a label have destroyed my social position, but it would also have affected my parents' standing in the community. In parochial Melbourne in the 1950s and 1960s a homosexual scandal would have gone around our social group very quickly.

But I doubt even if we had discussed my gender dysphoria that I would have personally related to being homosexual. Despite the fact that I considered myself a girl, I was attracted sexually to girls not to boys or men. Without my knowing it, my sexuality was actually lesbian, not heterosexual or male homosexual. At the time, being transgendered was not an option that

I knew of.

One of my fondest wishes now is that my mother had spoken to me about all this when I was a teenager, even if it could not be resolved, if only to make me think seriously about myself, to make me watch for possible answers or options. I regret that I was left totally ignorant. I was even naive enough to think that I was in control and could stop what I was doing any time I wanted to. With this erroneous belief I didn't see that I had a major problem. I enjoyed what I was doing. No one had told me I was doing wrong, although it was intimated. And I could stop at any time I wanted, I thought. Why worry?

When I wore women's clothes, underwear was always my first preference because I could have it on under my own clothes as I did homework or when I was not likely to be interrupted. I would quietly raid a drawer, go to the bathroom, change my clothes and then flush the toilet to ensure my cover. Going back to my room I'd return to my homework. My mother's stockings, her underpants and sometimes at bed time a nightie, were my favorites. I was caught again and again by my mother but the feeling that I was meant to be a girl was so strong that I was prepared to take whatever risks were necessary. The pleasure that the clothes gave me was always mitigated by the knowledge that if I was caught I would not be approved of.

I also had the feeling that when I was wearing women's underwear people could see through the heavy flannel school pants I normally wore. One night I went through the bathroom routine, putting on stockings and a suspender belt under my long pants, before coming down to the kitchen while dinner was being cooked. I sat around trying to be relaxed but I was so sure everyone could see the sheer stockings that I only lasted about five minutes before I had to go back upstairs and take them off.

All my cross-dressing was normally done at home. Only rarely did I wear my mother's underwear to school. On one occasion I picked a day when there was no sport scheduled and off I went. But there was an unexpected cross-country running practice after school. This would have required me to change in front of sixty or seventy boys, to have stripped down to my lace-trimmed panties in front of my class mates and put on shorts and sneakers. I refused, without giving any reason other than I did not want to do sport that afternoon. "Go to the locker-room and change!" I was told by one of the senior boys. The next day I had to answer to my teacher and ended up with a detention.

On another occasion I wore one of my sister's singlets to school. It was made of white cotton, similar to my own, but had a scalloped neck-line trimmed with white satin ribbon, tied in a bow in front. I went undetected.

Another time was the first day of term when I was in fifth-form, aged sixteen. I 'borrowed' a pair of yellow cotton under-pants with a nice lace trimming around the legs from my mother's drawer and went off to school. At the morning assembly the headmaster got up to say that two of the boys from the boarding house "had disgraced themselves, their families and the school during the previous term and would not be coming back." They had been caught one night "together in the same bed." I knew that what I was doing would also mean probable expulsion if I were caught so I rarely cross-dressed at school again.

For me this continuous desire to cross-dress was never anything more than an outward expression of my desire to be seen as a girl or woman. It was not sexual, nor was it an act of revolt against authority. I did it purely for the satisfaction of seeing myself in a feminine role and for the brief enjoyment of seeing my outward appearance and my true sex as I knew it could be united.

All this time I was desperately scared someone would find out that I was different. I reasoned that the biggest risk of this happening would be if anyone got to know me. I believed that as long as my friends or teachers were kept at a distance then I would be safe. I ended up with only a few close friends, and none close enough to confide in.

Scholastically I tried to achieved anonymity by becoming average. I reasoned that as long as I was not at the top or bottom then no one would take an interest in me. This worked well most of the time at school, except in my last two years when I came very close to failing. My teachers tried to get me to improve my marks by using scare tactics, like telling me I would never succeed in the world if I did not work harder.

In sport I was always among the last picked for a team, which suited me as I hated organized games like football and cricket. If I was forced to play I would try to get a position as far from the action as possible. In football this was at the full-forward position. I was normally on a losing team and so it was rare for us to get the ball anywhere near our own goal. I could just stand there and look as though I was participating, trotting backward and forward in mock anticipation of action, praying that the ball would not come near me. When it occasionally did I raced forward, feigning enthusiasm, all the while ensuring that I paced myself so as to reach the ball just a moment or two after someone else did.

Since participation in sport was compulsory I could not avoid it completely but I did the best I could. I stuck to non-team and non-contact sport where possible, like tennis or cross-country running. The best I ever did at sport was rowing because I was light and could be the coxswain. I rose to be cox of the 'house eight' but no higher as I did not like giving orders to people. I couched all my commands as requests, and used no authority in my voice.

"Okay? Sit forward. Are you Ready? Row?" I'd yell.

We won quite a few races but I would never demand my crew give more, I always felt sorry for them as they grew red in the face and started to sway and miss strokes from fatigue.

Socially I mixed with others who were also average and never became a close friend with anyone other than the boy who lived next door to me, and one other. I played with them, and later drank with them, yet even though they were my closest friends I never dreamed of talking to them about my need to live as a girl. I was too scared of being ostracized.

Through my teenage years I cross-dressed regularly but only

for short periods at a time—five minutes here, an hour there. The longest time span was on those nights when I took a nightie from the dirty linen basket and slept in it. I learned to use dirty clothes because I could just put them back in the laundry after wearing them. I would sneak out to the laundry, roll up a nightie and put it under my sweater, and go straight to my room, to bed. I reasoned there was less chance of being caught this way. Someone might notice their clean clothes missing from a drawer but not their dirty laundry.

To play with dolls also required hiding them and making sure I was alone when I took them out. Ironically my sisters were not very interested in their dolls. They never missed them when I took them. Under the pretense of needing to study, I closed my door, set the dolls on my bed and talked to them, dressed them, and acted out various dramatic fantasies. When I finished I looked for somewhere to hide them. Sometimes I put them behind the curtain on the window ledge, never thinking that, from this hiding spot, they were completely visible to anyone looking at my window from the outside.

All this time I still had the feeling that I was growing up as two people— a boy that the world knew and the little girl that only I knew. I did all the things my peers did and spent many happy days riding bikes, building cubby-houses, exploring local building sites and generally behaving like any well-adjusted young boy. When we traveled my father taught me how to use a gun and when we stayed on my uncle's farm I rode with him in the old Land Rover as he checked the sheep and fences. In general I was content with my lifestyle. When my mind was occupied for long periods with the whirl of life and growing up I didn't think of myself in relation to gender or sexuality. I just enjoyed life as any child does. But there was always my secret lurking in the background.

I had two younger sisters while I was a teenager, but I don't think they knew what I was doing. They were as sexually naive as I was and they never caught me playing with their dolls or cross-dressing. The older one, Mandy, was out-going and adventurous and I often felt jealous that I could not stand up to my parents the way she did. She had many confrontations with them and she fought when I would have just hung my head and backed away to sulk. Mandy was also very sport-minded, always riding her horse or playing softball for her school team.

Sally, was seven years younger than me. She was the achiever in the family, liked by the teachers, got good marks at school and went on to do a tertiary level course in veterinary science, the first in the family to get beyond secondary school.

Christmas and birthdays were always hard yet, like every child, I had high expectations of such events. Every year until I was fourteen or fifteen I woke at first light and sneaked slowly down the spiral staircase to the bottom step to see if any presents were in the pillow cases we had left under the tree the night before. The family rule was that we all went downstairs together. I rationalized that 'downstairs' meant on the carpet downstairs and that standing on the last step of the stairs was not being downstairs. From this vantage point, if I held on with one hand and swung way out on one foot, I could see around the corner and into the living room. In the far corner in front of the window was the artificial tree covered in decorations and tinsel. On a table beside it was the remains of a glass of milk and biscuits we had left out for Father Christmas. Under the tree were the brightly wrapped presents from friends and relations. The pillow cases we had put out the night before with our names pinned to them were standing nearby, misshapen by the presents Father Christmas had left.

I scuttled back up, scared with excitement that someone would catch me. I lay in bed with my heart pounding, waiting for what seemed forever until the hour when I could race into my parent's bedroom and announce that it was Christmas morning.

"It's seven o'clock, can we go down?"

"Go and wake your sisters while we get a cup of tea," my mother said.

"All right but come quickly," I replied and ran to wait impatiently at the top of the stairs.

Slowly the rest of the family got up and headed toward the stairs where we would collect until all were present, and then we went down as a family. My mother usually brought up the rear, carrying her large boat of a tea cup, decorated with red Chinese figures crossing a little bridge.

Each Christmas my father's mother, Nana B, would give my sisters and me a gift of clothing. One year she evidently got the labels mixed up. When I opened my gift, instead of the usual, boring blue school shirts, there was a white party dress with blue ribbon trim. My heart soared for an instant, then my mother took the box from me, with the dress still in it, and said that there had obviously been a mistake—this was for my sister. She handed me another box which had, as usual, my boring blue school shirts in it. I was heart-broken. For one delicious moment I thought that my family had found out my secret and that from then on I was going to be recognized by them as a girl.

I waited every Christmas morning thereafter hoping that one day I would be given a white party dress of my own.

Chapter Three

It was my lesbianism that really hid from everyone, including myself, the fact that I was transgendered. I just thought that I was a normal heterosexual boy, very sad and confused for most of the time by what I considered a perverted need to wear women's clothes and be a girl. If I had been attracted to boys or men, I would probably have come to see myself as homosexual. I had heard of this option and therefore had a standard to judge myself against: boy plus boy equals homosexual. Being lesbian-transgendered I had no such standard to measure against: boy (even though he believes he is a girl) plus girl equals heterosexual. I didn't know that there was a third option: transgendered boy plus girl equals lesbian-transgendered.

The closest I came to any sort of homosexual contact occurred when I was about nineteen. I went to the hotel regularly with a group of friends and one evening one of them said he had met an older man who was a 'poofter,' but who had some wonderful paintings in his Toorak house. If we wanted to he could take us around and get us in for a look at them.

It was a bit of a dare and my friends said that they would go on the theory that, if there were more than one of us, he would not try to come-on to anyone. Not wanting to be left out of the group, I went along. I have no idea what I expected, perhaps the stereotyped effeminate man with a cravat and doused in perfume, but the man was not outstanding to look at in his gray pants and white shirt. The house was unimposing and as we were lead from room to room I was not impressed by the paintings. As far as I was concerned the whole evening was rather a non-event. Afterwards my friends and I had a teenage discussion about what 'poofters' did to each other.

I thought about this visit often and turned it into another one of my fantasies: I would go to him and he would buy me a wardrobe full of girl's clothes. I would come to his house on weekends and after school and be treated as a real woman. I could see myself, swanning around his house in perfect acceptance and security, because I knew he could not tell anyone about me without revealing himself.

I never acted on this fantasy. I just added it to all my other ones.

As a teenager, some of the best opportunities for me to submerge myself in a private world of fantasy came at parties. I looked on these social events in various ways. First, everyone went to them. I had to go. Second, they allowed me to be with a group of friends and have a few drinks, usually too many, and party. But they also put me in a position to enjoy the final and best reason for going: they gave me the vicarious opportunity to be a girl in public. I looked at the clothes the girls were wearing, enjoyed their conversations and shared in their femininity, all without the risk of it being discovered that I too was a girl.

The parties were normally organized by parents to celebrate things such as birthdays or the end of the school year. Beer was served, mainly for the boys, as it was felt that this was a safe drink, as was sherry for the girls. There was also a large bowl of fruit punch and plenty of chips. Music was from the 45s and 33LPs played on the family radiogram in the corner.

When I arrived I selected one girl and pretended I was her for the night. I watched her and fantasized that it was me in that dress with the low shoulders, wearing make-up and having hair that swept my shoulders. It was me laughing and dancing with ease. What I really wanted at this age, in the late 1960s, was to go to a party in a full skirt, or a dress with layered petticoats (which would have looked pretty silly as the fashions had by this time moved to mini skirts). I craved growing breasts and having a period, a different set of life expectations heaped upon me. It was the physical attributes of being a woman that I wanted. My life would have been very different, maybe no better or worse than what I had, but it would have been a life inestimably less confusing for me.

Often my taste in clothing was not that of my friends, male or female. I dreamed of wearing the extremes in fashion. At one eighteenth birthday party a girl came in a very frilly and be-ribboned dress, all white with wide blue satin bows, white bobby-sox and black patent leather shoes. The overall effect was like one of the sketches of Alice from *Alice in Wonderland*.

People groaned and whispered to each other, "Why would her mother dress her that way. Surely it's not her own taste."

I looked at her and sighed to myself, "If only my mother would dress me like that!"

I could be very jealous of girls at a party and often went home either very drunk or very depressed. Normally, though, I spent my time inconspicuously at the back of the room, alone or with one or two others, with a glass of beer in my hand, while everyone else danced.

It was during these years that I discovered another problem. I was not accepted by girls as another girl. One September holiday we were staying with friends on a sheep station in South Australia. There was a party at an adjoining property to which we all went. As usual the children broke into two groups. The girls stayed inside and the boys went out to play football. I stayed inside to play with the girls but they teased me and called me a 'poofter' until finally I had to leave. I hated football so instead of going to join the boys I wandered off by myself and sat under a tree in the yard, near the sheep paddocks. Under a nearby bush was an echidna and I watched as it kicked at the ground with its short legs, digging a hole in the loosened sandy soil until it had buried itself and only the top of its spiny back was showing. I enjoyed watching the echidna but I still felt very lonely and dejected until it was time to go home.

I enjoyed being with girls sexually, although I was very naive and shy. During and after parties my sexual contact was limited to kissing and hugging, but I looked forward to it. I could fantasize that I was a girl, being kissed by a girl. In the dark, or with my eyes closed, my masculine appearance was invisible to me and I could mentally deny its existence. Beyond kissing and hugging I had no physical interest in sexual contact with girls.

The whole period was very confusing for me sexually. I was physically and emotionally attracted to the girls I knew and wanted to be with them, but I had no interest in playing the dominant role that I felt was expected of me, and I had no interest in intercourse. I couldn't admit this without opening myself up to derision by my friends. As a result I led an asexual lifestyle and withdrew even more from close contact with my friends.

Emotionally, being transgendered made it very uncomfortable for me to join in, or even listen to my friends on those occasions when they bragged of their sexual conquests. It was painful to sit and listen to how they had got some girl drunk, or tricked her in some way, into having sex with them. Even when the girl had been a willing participant their comments were often cruel as they impressed each other with their prowess. If it was a one night stand, they branded the girl 'an easy fuck.' Listening to all this made me feel like a spy, or a traitor, in their midst. I tolerated what they said, and even sometimes fabricated some story of my own, all to hide the fact that I felt that I was a girl too. Mostly I sat silently, listening as they insulted their girlfriends.

I prayed regularly that I would be involved in an accident that would sever my penis and allow me to enter the ranks of women. Many years later when I went for a vasectomy I hoped the doctor might slip and castrate me. He didn't—worst luck. My need to live as female was so intense, yet I did not have the knowledge or courage to do anything about it.

After I got my driver's license all sorts of opportunities opened up, but I was never brave enough to take full advantage of them. The best I did was trips to our Portsea house by myself. I told my parents that I wanted to have a quiet weekend alone. The house was an hour and a half drive south of Melbourne and set on a large double block of land. On arriving I went for a long walk across the adjoining golf course, or along the deserted ocean beach to do some bird watching. I took binoculars and scanned the sea looking for albatross, which were fairly common, and watched the gannets as they folded their wings and dove down to the water like white javelins. Back at the house I checked through the cupboards for suitable clothes and then settled down for a feminine evening of brightly printed cotton sun-dresses.

The year I left Melbourne Grammar was the first year of quotas at Victorian universities. With my bare pass in five subjects I could not get into a subject that my parents deemed suitable, such as accounting or law. My mother actively discouraged me from trying one of the interstate universities which would have accepted me with my pass level. She also attempted to keep my two sisters at home for as long as possible too. None of us were encouraged to try our wings and live away from home.

So I remained living at home through my teens and twenties and got into the habit of drinking heavily every night. On weekends I went away with friends. I had a very heterosexual lifestyle of drinking-parties, ski weekends, and later sailing. It was all good fun at the time, though very self destructive. Between the age of eighteen and twenty-eight it was a rare night for me not to have at least one large bottle of beer and three or four glasses of wine before I went to bed. Normally I got home at about 5 p.m, drank beer until dinner, drank wine until I went to bed, which was usually between 10 and 11 p.m. Our house gained quite a reputation for its convivial atmosphere and friends would drop in on their way home from work or after dinner to join in our nightly 'kitchen party.'

With hindsight, I see that my failure to go on to tertiary education shielded me from possible relationships and contacts that may have broadened my understanding of myself. I could have found people or books that could have activated my search for wholeness many years before I finally started looking. I would have been thrown into the social awareness of university in the mid 1960s. I would have entered a world much wider than my sheltered, middle-class, white Anglo-Saxon existence.

Instead of going to university, I started a job with the accounting company of Price Waterhouse and met my first friends outside of school. One of my co-workers, Ian, introduced me the joy of skiing. He was a member of a lodge at Mount Buller and from then on I went skiing most weekends during winter. Those weekends involved lots of heavy drinking as well as skiing and I looked forward to them. I would pack my Fiat 600 on Friday morning and leave for the slopes straight from work. The drive took four hours and I arrived at about 10 p.m., got drunk, and went to bed. Saturday morning I would be out skiing when the lifts opened and I'd stay until they closed for the night. I'd stop for drinks on my way home.

Some of the commercial lodges in those days were unlicensed and would serve red wine in coffee cups in case they were raided. This was a common practice in the mid 1960s and some of the unlicensed Melbourne cafés did the same thing.

After an evening of drinking I'd attempt to ski back to the lodge. The slopes were not groomed so there were small bushes sticking through the snow and an occasional depression where a stream crossed the run, exposing a muddy hole of rocks and grass. In daylight these traps were easy enough to navigate but when drunk at night it became a real challenge. Back at the lodge I would have dinner with many more drinks and then collapse into bed in the small hours of the morning. Some mornings I woke with absolutely no memory of how I had gotten to bed, or when. I then skied all day Sunday and finally left in the late afternoon for the drive home and work on Monday. While I worked for Price Waterhouse I followed the same scenario every weekend of the ski season.

Those skiing excursions showed me, for the first time, what it was like to be away from home and parental supervision. They allowed me to drink heavily and take on a macho role, which I quickly recognized as being as good a disguise for my transgenderism as my earlier escape into mediocrity had been. Who would ever guess that this hard-drinking, bearded he-man was really a woman in disguise? Perfect.

Sadly, I did not exchange my earlier role of mediocrity for my new macho image; I just added to it. My skiing, which I loved, never developed enough to be more than proficient. At work I drifted along doing just enough to ensure that I was not fired, but I never found the need to excel. And both my work and my recreation put me in a situation where I could drink heavily and drift more quickly toward becoming an alcoholic.

I stayed with Price Waterhouse for two years and failed my accounting exams the three times I sat them. The situation was not helped by the fact that I was taking classes after work. I became good friends with the owner of a small cafe near the school where I would get a meal before going to an auditing or accounting class. He would bring me glasses of red wine to try with my meal. By the time I left for class I was more interested in sleeping than learning.

I was not interested in accounting enough to worry when the books didn't balance. Once I got them to within a dollar or two, I felt that that was close enough, but I'd persevere until they balanced because I knew it was required. I did not enjoy the challenge or the work.

I left Price Waterhouse when my father offered me a job in the engineering company he had bought a few years earlier. I remained in the job for four years as accountant and general assistant, and also learned how to weld, use a lathe, produce engineering drawings and work with people as a manager. During those years I learned a lot of practical skills but did not finish any formal education in any of them.

I was also very interested in cars, my first being a 1928 Chevrolet tourer that I bought when I was sixteen. This was followed by a series of Fiat sedans for everyday use, and vintage cars as a hobby. Among the vintage cars were a 1921 Diatto and a 1949 MG TC, both of which I bought to restore. Neither restoration was completed before I sold the cars for one reason or another. Later on, when I lived at Officer outside Melbourne, I bought an electric-blue Daimler SP 250 which had a V8 motor.

My interest in cars was twofold. First, I admired them for their aesthetic qualities, their stylish lines and the precision engineering that was required to make them. Second, and just as important at the time, they were a prestige item that made me feel I had credibility amongst my friends. They were good for my self esteem and when I drove them I felt as though some of their macho image rubbed off on me. I could drive them fast and feel as though I was seen in the eyes of my peers as a "real man."

My need to be perceived as a man, mixed with my heavy drinking led one night to my having a serious car accident. I left the Cruising Yacht Club of Australia dinner after midnight to drive down to the club where I sailed from. I was going to sleep on board the yacht to be ready for the racing on the next day. About half way to the club I lost control of my car in a corner at high speed. It careered off the road, across the footpath, took out some small road-side trees, then swerved violently back onto the road across the path of the traffic. I have no memory of what happened next but I hit an on-coming car head on.

The passenger in my car was rushed to hospital with serious head injuries and my car was totaled. Thankfully my friend lived and recovered and the occupants of the other car were not injured. After being tested with a blood-alcohol reading of 0.15, I ended up in court and lost my license. It was purely good fortune that I did not kill someone, but the accident did not curb my drinking.

Denial was still playing a major part in my life. I was trying anything to hide my femininity, even from myself. My whole life revolved around the effort. I drank heavily, partied hard and drove too fast. I wanted to be seen as a man. My clothing could not show any color. I didn't say words like 'pretty.' I was petrified that someone would guess my true feelings. Whatever it took to prove to myself and others that I was one hundred percent male, I did. But I still felt like an interloper among my friends. I felt that I had to prove to them that I was a man. I worked at trying to achieve what those around me never questioned. I went through all this effort because I wanted to fit in. I was doing everything in my power to force myself into the role allotted to me—yet at the same time I wanted even more to be allowed to live as the woman I knew I was.

One outward sign of my masculinity was my beard. From old photos I can tell now how I was feeling at the time by whether or not I had a beard. With a beard I was playing a macho role. I was proving that I could do it; it made me look older and more rugged. Without the beard, the younger, feminine me was at the fore. At these times I would be welcoming her into my life and expressing her in my desires and hidden wardrobe of clothes.

I was not alone in my attempts to hide my feminine self. I know of transgendered people who have been submarine officers, combat helicopter pilots and interstate truck drivers, all trying to prove that they were men. All of them were trying to prove to themselves and society that they were something they were not. I took up ocean yacht racing and sailed over twenty thousand miles, including five Sydney-Hobart races, the first Melbourne to Hobart west coast race, a Fastnet race in England and numerous shorter races and cruises in England, America and Australia.

Despite the fact that I initially took up sailing to prove my manhood I grew to love it and became immersed in it to the point that I stopped going skiing and spent every weekend and most Wednesday evenings for more than eight years either sailing or working on the boat. I enjoyed it immensely and would not have missed any of it.

There is something romantic and sensual about the sea. The creaking and straining of a small yacht is a very special feeling. The ocean is so subtle and powerful, full of potential danger, and yet I always felt safe on it. I felt that it was infinitely old and knowledgeable and that it knew how frail we were. It seemed to surround me with strength and beauty and provide a solitude and security I have rarely found elsewhere. While sailing I could just be me. I could immerse myself in all the beauty and forget that I was different. My time was taken up by watching sea birds and the sails, or the role of the waves as we passed across their surface. For the duration of the trip I was in another world, one which absorbed all my attention and imagination.

One of the most beautiful trips I ever took was the return trip from a Sydney-Hobart race in 1971. At that time I was sailing as fore-deck hand on a yacht called *Salacia* which was owned by

Fred Thomas, the man who was to become my father-in-law. We sailed slowly up the East Coast of Tasmania stopping at the fishing village of Triabunna. In Wine Glass Bay the water was so clear that we could see down 10 meters to the bottom and watch sand-crabs crawl into our make-shift net before we pulled them to the surface for dinner that night. The boat was well stocked and we sat on the deck in the warm evening air drinking chilled wine and eating fresh-boiled sand-crabs. The next day we sailed with a steady southwest wind to Flinders Island where we anchored for the night.

The next morning we met a cray fishing boat whose skipper traded us five crayfish, one for each of us, in exchange for two bottles of red wine. The morning was calm and sunny with a light following breeze and not a cloud in sight. We cruised gently along under a large blue and red spinnaker with the boat slightly rocking on a small ocean swell as we ate the crays, with more chilled white wine.

The weather remained calm and that evening as we sailed north the full moon came up ahead of us and spread a silver path on the water ahead. In the light of this reflected path phosphorescent plankton swirled from our bow, turning our bow-wave into a silver, flashing cape for our boat. As it rose higher, the moon shone through the spinnaker, backlighting it and casting shadows from the rigging and cabin-top onto the deck. I brought a half empty bottle of port on deck, threw the cork over the side, and Fred and I sat together drinking and talking into the small hours of the morning until we reached Wilsons Promontory and Refuge Cove where we anchored.

From there we sailed west through more islands, 'The Glennies,' and past the romantically named 'Skull Rock,' which is a round, barren dome with a large weathered hole in one side about the size of a house. The story goes that sailing ships used to try and fire cannon balls into the hole for target practice. We spent one more night anchored in Warratah Bay and then sailed back through 'the heads' into Port Phillip Bay and up to Melbourne.

Other trips were not so idyllic. My first ocean race, in the *Winston Churchill*, a 16-meter wooden boat that had sailed in the first Sydney-Hobart race in 1945 and many other ocean races as well, including a Trans-Pacific, we nearly sank. It was a race from Melbourne to Portland in early November 1968, at the end of the winter storm season, and we were hit by a violent southwesterly gale soon after the start. We had gone too far to consider returning, especially as the only real protection from the storm lay behind the arm of land extending into the sea at our destination, Portland.

The waves built steadily from the west, a long Antarctic swell adding to their size, before the full force of the wind hit us. For safety we had reefed the main down until it was no bigger than a postage stamp, then tied extra gaskets around it to make sure it didn't break free. The storm jib we put up was of old canvas and so thick and heavy that we said it was bullet-proof.

I became so sick that I prayed for the boat to sink. The thought of drowning promised nothing but peace and release from how I felt; I had absolutely no will to go on living. I could not even get on deck to help the rest of the crew, even though they were completely exhausted. By the time we reached port the boat was leaking through every seam and we had to pump to stay afloat.

At first I wanted to get a bus and return to Melbourne by road but I was talked into sailing back on the yacht, and so found the courage to go on and do more races, none of which where like that first.

At no time during those years of my early twenties did it ever occur to me that other people might feel the gender dysphoria that I felt. I had still not heard the word transgendered. I imagined that my feelings were just some quirk I had and that I could stop cross-dressing whenever I wanted to. I just never wanted to.

Chapter Four

It wasn't until 1973 when I turned twenty-seven and became engaged that my lack of interest in being sexually male and my need to live openly as a woman started to affect people outside my immediate family. No one had ever spoken to me about sexual matters, let alone transgenderism, and I had never gone asking or reading. I was still a virgin; and I also honestly still thought that Jennifer could be cast off forever, whenever I chose. I became engaged to Laurie, the daughter of my friend and yachting skipper Fred.

Her family was from America and her father, Fred, with whom I was sailing, was a director of an American company that had been sent out to run a new branch in Melbourne. Laurie went to high school in Melbourne but then went back to America and to college. She only came back to Australia during college vacations.

I met her once or twice during her visits. She would come down to the boat for a social sail. After the last Sydney to Hobart race we did, Laurie and her mother and sisters came to meet Fred and I when we arrived in dock. I spent some time with Laurie in Hobart and one night, after I had gotten extremely drunk, she helped me back to the boat. After that it was two months before I had the courage to contact her again. I finally called her to apologize and asked her to come out to dinner. She accepted and in the few months before she went back to college we went out regularly, including a long weekend trip to Wonboyn with some of my friends.

In April 1975 her family returned to America and in May I was asked by a friend, Warrick, who was part of the crew on *Salacia*, to crew on a 15-meter British yacht called *Synergy* in the Fastnet race in England. Since Laurie was traveling around Europe, I thought that this would be an excellent opportunity to see her, as well as some of England. I made plans and bought an around-the-world ticket so that after England I could visit America and spend more time with Laurie and her family on my way home.

We met up with Warrick in Southampton for the race. Afterwards we were told by the owner of the yacht that we could take it for two weeks to go cruising. This was too good an offer to turn down so Laurie, Warrick and I took the yacht and crossed to the Channel Islands and visited Sark and Alderney before returning the boat to Southampton. The weather for the whole trip was perfect. Our only expense for two weeks of luxury cruising on a 15-meter yacht was our food and drink.

Afterwards Laurie and I rented a car and drove up to Scotland to visit the highlands. Both our ancestors had come from that area. Laurie's family was from the West Coast and mine from the Northeast. Being on a budget we made good use of bed and breakfasts and cheap hotels. Some nights we slept cramped in the car, parked in a farm lane, and awoke cold and stiff to the sound of woodland birds.

We managed to get as far north as Scourie before running out of time and having to drive south again. Laurie caught a plane from Edinburgh to get back in time for the start of her last year of college.

It was a wonderful trip and Laurie and I developed an extremely close friendship. We both loved traveling and shared an avid interest in bird watching. Laurie also knew a lot about plants and flowers and introduced me to a wider level of interest in nature. I felt as though I had really met someone that I could spend the rest of my life with; but I also felt very inadequate and never imagined that she would want to live with me.

The night after she left I opened my bag and found a note

from her saying what a wonderful trip she had had and thanking me. I drove the hire-car back to London and, after getting lost in rush hour traffic around Marble Arch for an hour, found my way to Heathrow and caught the plane to New York from there.

I spent a weekend in New York wandering the streets in bemused shock at the noise and color. Central Park was alive with late summer activity. Jamaican drummers beat out fantastic rhythms and vendors sold hot dogs and pretzels. The pond had model yachts sailing back and forth. There were women pushing babies in black carriages with white sheets and pillows. Pigeons were everywhere and frisbees flew freely. At the top of one set of stairs a young boy sat with a set of scales selling drugs and a band played in the rotunda. I wandered through this magical scene enchanted but not brave enough to sample anything other than the scene, and the hot dogs.

I walked back down Fifth Avenue toward my hotel, browsing the used books being sold from carts along the wall of the park. Most of the books were novels but the top book on one pile was about homosexuality and transexualism. I picked it up and flicked furtively through it, slowly coming to the realization that it was written about people like me. I put it down in shock and walked on—but I couldn't stop thinking about what I had read in the few seconds in which I had held the book in my hands. There were other people in the world who felt as I did.

On Monday morning I took the train down to Washington where I stayed for a week with Laurie's parents and met up again with Warrick. We decided it would be fun to see some of the country and Laurie at Principia College in St. Louis. Our first plan was to buy a used car for a few hundred dollars and sell it again before we left. With the used car section of the paper in hand we walked to a yard near the middle of town where there was a large, pink Cadillac Fleetwood convertible. We fell in love, and pictured ourselves cruising down the interstate, radio playing, the wind blowing our hair. Sadly they wanted eight-hundred dollars for it, well beyond our reach.

In the end we compromised our dream and settled on practicality. We were offered the use of Laurie's parents' yellow Volkswagen bus. We accepted and drove it in a loop down through Tennessee and up to St. Louis, camping in the van as we went.

It was a wonderful trip through the Blue Ridge and Smoky Mountains National Parks and across Tennessee to St. Louis. I got my first taste of America on this trip and learned that it was not just a land of freeways and massive cities. The scenery was spectacular and we tried to keep to the minor roads as much as possible. We also found many cultural differences. We stopped to get a pot to cook sweet corn in. Walking into a small hardware store we asked the owner if he had any saucepans. He stared at us as if we were speaking a foreign language, which in fact we were. Australian English is nothing like rural Tennessee American English. It wasn't until I put on my best American accent and knowledge of television culture and asked for a "kook-in-part" that we got what we needed. Later we had a meal in an old-fashioned road house complete with wooden booths and men leaning on the bar who eyed us suspiciously. We ordered the special, chilly-beans, and a coke each and I eavesdropped on the conversation at the bar as best I could. It intrigued me to slowly come to the realization that all I knew about America was what I had learned about its economy at school and from Hollywood movies. I was seeing for the first time how people really lived. I was getting my first taste of how it might be to live in a country other than Australia, though I never expected that I would.

We spent about a week with Laurie at Principia in its beautiful rural campus and she introduced me to her friends, and to many of the spectacular birds in the area. She also invited Warrick and me to go on a canoe trip with her and some of her friends down the Current River. It wasn't white-water canoeing but, what with continuous rain and our total inexperience, we ended up very wet.

Warrick drove back to Washington, leaving me with Laurie to make my plans to fly back to Australia from St. Louis.

Laurie and I spent two more days together enjoying each other's company and the late summer weather before my flight home. On the last night, as we lay on mats in the deserted college gym listening to the rain on the roof, she proposed to me. I was taken totally by surprise as I did not think that anyone, especially someone as special as Laurie, could ever love me enough to want to marry me. As we lay there I said yes I would marry her and the next morning I climbed on the plane in a bemused daze. I loved her but marriage was not something I had really thought about. The more I did, the better the idea seemed.

I got back to Australia and that evening as we stood around in the kitchen drinking and waiting for dinner to cook I told my parents that I was engaged. The first words from my mother were, "Thank heavens, we thought you'd never do it."

"What do you mean?" I asked.

"Oh nothing," she said. "We are just happy you are getting married."

It may have been an innocent remark but I have always wondered if she believed I was homosexual.

The society I grew up in mandated that I, as an apparently heterosexual man, should marry. I believed this and I believed, at one level, that marriage would not be a problem as, in my extreme state of denial, I believed I could stop cross-dressing whenever I wanted to. I also felt that marriage would cure me of what I had been taught by society to believe were my 'perverted needs and delusions;' my delusion that I was a woman.

The more honest part of me, the part of me that was Jennifer, knew that I would always strive to be a woman. Deep down I wanted to marry a woman so that I could live with her and be her closest friend, her partner, and share life together. Jennifer's fantasy of marriage was to enter into something that would approximate, for her, a lesbian relationship.

I was still living at home and, apart from one brief period of a month when I moved into a flat with a friend from school, I never lived away from home and was, in many ways, socially ignorant. Now I was involving a whole new family in my dysphoric life. I could not warn them nor give them the option as to whether or not they wanted to join it; I was too scared. Also, I honestly thought that marriage would bring an end to my feelings of femininity and my desire to wear dresses. Marriage would prove my manliness.

The night before I left for America to get married I took one of my mother's nighties from the dirty clothes basket. Climbing into bed I said to myself that this would be the last time that I ever wore women's clothes. This was the last time forever; it was a farewell party.

Laurie and I were married in the backyard of her parents' Washington house in July 1974. I had flown over at the end of June and my parents and sisters arrived just before the wedding before traveling on to England and Italy. A few friends also came over and they used the chance to travel on to Europe afterwards as well.

We had planned to get married in a small country church in Bethesda, Maryland. The church looked as if it were straight out of a tourist book. It had tall trees in front of it and a white picket fence. It sat on a slight rise beside a small country road and was painted white, inside and out, with polished wooden pews. I could picture the early settlers, in long dresses and bonnets, leaving in horse drawn buggies and carriages after the Sunday service.

We met with the minister and made all the arrangements for what would be a traditional wedding, complete with organ music and a sense of history. As the minister said farewell to us from the front steps of his church, he asked if we were planning on having any "Negro" guests.

"Yes," we said. "We are planning on having some Black friends at the wedding, Why?"

"In that case, the ceremony cannot be held in this church," he said. "I don't mind, of course, but some of my parishioners wouldn't like it if Negroes came into their church."

It was my first taste of discrimination. In my ignorance I had never realized that racial discrimination was practiced so blatantly, even within the church. We canceled the arrangements with the church and arranged a backyard wedding.

As it turned out, it was a beautiful wedding with flowers in our hair and Laurie carrying a bouquet of wildflowers that she and her sisters had picked that morning. The day was a clear, humid Washington summer day and we all stood around before the ceremony chatting. The minister arrived wearing a beautiful handmade white chasuble that reached to the grass and was covered in multi-colored letters and patterns. It shone in the sun.

The party afterwards went on well into the evening, after we had left to spend our wedding night in a hotel in Georgetown. Unfortunately there was no time for us to have a honeymoon as I had to get back to Australia and work. We flew out two days later and set up home in a small terrace house I had bought for us in Port Melbourne.

I was now sharing a house and a bedroom and could not just hide something in a drawer or get dressed without being seen. I was sharing my life now, and to do this one needs to be honest and open. Sadly, I could be neither without wrecking the marriage, and my marriage had not killed my femininity.

Soon after we returned to Australia the desire to be seen and accepted as a woman resurfaced. What could I do? It was winter and I worked in an old, unheated factory so I asked Laurie if I could wear some pantyhose, just for the warmth. She said I could and gave me an old pair of hers. I started dropping hints about how much more comfortable I felt women's underpants were than men's.

The old habits and needs were back. To make it worse I did not grasp the depth of anguish my ignorance and denial caused. For me, I was living with a woman in what for all intents and purposes was, by my definition, a lesbian relationship.

It was a relationship where I could express and explore my feminine feelings with a woman I loved. I felt supported at home and worked in my job to give our relationship the ability to grow. I did not know any lesbians at the time so I could not measure my day to day relationship in my marriage with the reality of the world, but I knew as surely as I ever had that I was not interested in having sex with men.

Being married also gave me the psychological excuse to do something I had never done before: buy women's clothing for myself. I could go into a shop and pretend to be interested in finding a gift for my wife. I could look at hankies and other options and then settle on buying underwear, graciously accepting the shop assistants offer to gift wrap it.

The first time I bought anything was about six months after we were married. I kept it very basic and free of lace or detailing and told Laurie I only wore it because it was more comfortable. After awhile Laurie said she did not approve of my feminine underwear and it had to go. I sensed her tension without realizing how deeply she felt about it. I see now that I was selfish and insensitive, but at the time I was confused. I wanted to be seen as a woman, but didn't want to destroy the marriage.

I had no idea how to talk to anyone, especially Laurie, about how I felt. I believed that to talk to her would be the end of the marriage. To talk to anyone else would lead to the end of my social status. Either way I believed I would lose everything, and I was not strong enough to do it. I ended up feeling disgusted with myself and retreating back to the 'cupboard.' I lied and told her it was not important to me and so into the rubbish the underwear went.

This pattern went on for some years with us both slowly, over sixteen years, coming to the realization that I would never stop.

Through the years I tried desperately to find someone who would see me as a woman and accept me. I did not try very hard to hide my women's clothes. I did not wear them for any sexual purpose but purely for what they represented to me at the time. They represented the outer badge of the group I wanted to belong to. Clothes were the outward sign of my inner needs. They were, unfortunately, also the 'red rags' that aroused so much passion.

Clothes also plotted my violent pendulum-like swings over the years between trying to conform to societal and family pressures to be male and my own need to live as a woman. As I slowly explored and found my feelings and needs, the variety of clothes I bought expanded. I went from underwear to skirts and dresses. This escalation in clothing was matched by an escalation in the emotional intensity of the verbal fights that Laurie and I ended up in. I stumbled through excuses, too afraid to express my true feelings, and Laurie struggled with the frustration and fear of not knowing where our relationship was going and what failing in herself was driving me to this behavior. After each showdown I apologized profusely, through gales of tears, swearing "never again." I took all my clothes to the Salvation Army clothing drop. Over a fourteen year period, until near the end of our marriage when I started hiding clothes around the house, this pattern occurred many times and through my lack of courage it was never resolved until the end.

This was also the 1970s era of the caftan, and I bought two dressing gowns in this style. While they were ostensibly a unisex garment, to me they were pseudo-dresses. I would come home, shower and put one on. They were the one item that, when all else was gone, I could wear with some degree of tolerance from Laurie. She and I both knew that they were substituting for dresses but it was not discussed and I kept wearing them. The only time we spoke openly about my gender dysphoria was when I was caught cross-dressing. We didn't have a logical discussion, just a series of threats on Laurie's behalf and empty promises on mine. Between outbreaks we did not discuss my cross-dressing. I was scared of the consequences of rational discussion, and I assume Laurie was just praying, as my mother had, that it would all just go away in time.

One of good things for me in our marriage was that Laurie did not drink. I did not stop drinking but the only time I drank more than a glass of wine or beer was if we went out with friends or if I returned to my parents house and fell back into the old patterns. As a result the amount I drank decreased enormously.

In 1976, after about a year and a half of marriage, we decided to move to America to try a new life experience. As much as anything else the move was brought on by the stress my transgenderism was causing us. Our hope, though it was still unspoken between us, was that if we moved away from the social environment I had grown up in then maybe I could change, and leave my need to be a woman behind.

We packed our bags and arranged for a friend to house-sit for us until we could contact him and arrange to sell our house. We did this because we were not sure how long we would end up staying, and whether we would buy a house in America or just rent.

Laurie was more adventurous than me in many ways and decided that the way we should get to America was via Russia. She made many calls and found that if we flew to Japan we could get to Karbarovsk, on the far-east coast of Asian-Russia and then catch the Trans-Siberian Railway to Moscow.

We made our bookings and flew out of Australia in early October. In Russia we were booked to travel soft class, their equivalent of our first class, which meant we had our own double berth on the train rather than sharing a six-bunked cabin with four others.

The train was pulled by a steam locomotive that looked as though it was straight out of a 1920s movie. The carriages, though basically clean, appeared to be of the same vintage. Food was cooked on the train but we soon took to buying extras whenever we stopped. Food was in short supply in the east of the country and the train had taken on provisions in Moscow before it left but was now, on the return trip, running out of most things. Dinner was often a reasonable borscht followed by a dubious looking stew made of vegetables and meat from a cooler under the dirty floor of the kitchen, where it was exposed to the cold air of the moving train. Early in the trip it was possible to buy chocolate on the train, and we supplemented this with the excellent strong, black tea from the samovar in our carriage. This samovar was always full and guarded over by the *babushka* who was in charge of the carriage.

As always when traveling we had a wonderful trip. We never disagreed on what we should see or where we should go. Our tastes were very similar, except in food. Where I would try anything at least once, Laurie was more restrained. For example I was happy to just close my mind to what might be in the sometimes dubious looking meals on the train, while Laurie resorted to buying cabbages from vendors who crowded around the train each time it stopped, and eating them raw in our compartment. She was never sure when she would get another one, and she rationed herself to a few leaves a day, gradually whittling the vegetable down to its core.

From Moscow we took a train to Leningrad and then flew out to Oslo. From there we flew to New York where we were met by Laurie's parents. They were living in Darien, Connecticut, and after staying with them for a while, we started looking for somewhere to live nearby. We finally found a house about a half hour drive from them in Shelton, on the Housatonic River.

I did not know what to do for employment so, because of my love of sailing and a need for money, I went down to the local boat harbor and found a job cleaning and laboring in the yard of one of the yacht dealers. I did this for a season and learned the basics of fiber glass repair and spray painting. The next season I told my employer that I could do the spray painting job for him, and took over from the person who had taught me, as he had left the previous fall and not returned. He had been an excellent spray painter but had a drinking problem. The only way he could stop his hand from shaking while painting was to drink a quarter of a bottle of vodka before starting.

I ended up doing all the damage repair on boats in the yard, as well as detailing and respraying yachts for their owners. The largest boats I worked on were the ocean racing and cruising boats and those were up to twenty meters long and worth between one hundred and fifty and five hundred thousand dollars each. One owner paid two hundred thousand dollars for a new boat but did not like the shade of blue it had been built in. I had to sand down the whole boat and re-spray it a darker shade for him.

After I left the yard I went into business for myself repairing and spraying boats. I found the work satisfying as it allowed me to do fine detail work and return something damaged or worn to its original condition. I was creating something beautiful, rather than just trying to get a column of figures to add up as I had been doing in all my other jobs. I could stand back at the end of the day and see something tangible that I had done.

We stayed in Connecticut for about three years and, throughout this time, my normal patterns of trying to control my gender dysphoria continued, as did my wearing of women's clothes. The main difference now was that, because of the heavy outer-wear needed to ward off the cold during winter, there was more scope for my wearing women's underwear without being discovered. The trauma this caused in me was the need to be more careful of physical contact with Laurie in case she felt something unexpected, like the smooth slip of nylon underpants against nylon stockings. The need for feminine expression put a huge mental strain on me. My body language conveyed my tension to her as well but sadly we still never discussed what was happening.

During this period there was a degree of knowing and tolerance on both our parts. I knew that she knew I was wearing women's underwear, but I tried not to put her in a situation where she would see it. She knew what I was doing but rarely confronted me on the matter. It was only on those occasions where I was careless, or some other tension in our lives brought my cross-dressing to the fore that anything was said, and always by her, never me. I would, as always, apologize profusely, promise to change my habits.

As the marriage progressed I steadily lost interest in the sexual side of our relationship. I had little enough interest initially but as I slowly came to realize that I was not going to lose my desire to live openly as a woman, I gave up all attempts to become a man and play that role. This was not just a matter of liking or disliking dominant or submissive roles or passive or aggressive ones. It had nothing to do with socially constructed behavior: I just did not enjoy the physical act itself. I did not want to have a penis and use it sexually. I wanted a vagina and to be physically loved as and by a woman. The solution that I came up with that allowed me some degree of enjoyment from intercourse was to fantasize that I had female sex organs, that I was a lesbian.

I did not know any lesbians at the time and if I had I would not have asked how they made love any more than I would have asked any of my heterosexual friends about sex. I rarely discussed sex with my male friends as a boy at school, as a teenager or later in life. My parents had not said a word on the subject. I had never bought X-rated magazines or gone to porn movies. What I knew about sex I found out during marriage. The rest, I imagined. After experimentation I found out that I did not enjoy intercourse unless I could fantasize being a woman in bed with a woman. The political and social elements of the word lesbian were unknown. To me, what I did and how I felt became my definition of sexually being 'a lesbian.'

Despite the regularly recurring strain of my gender dysphoria Laurie and I did a lot of things together and lived a wonderful life. We were both keen on travel and on conservation issues. We joined the local Audubon Society and the Nature Conservancy, for which we did some site-evaluations of nature reserves and submitted reports to various bodies on land use recommendations. We also traveled throughout New England and had some exquisite camping holidays at places such as Mt. Katahdin in northern Maine. One particular spring we were the first people to hike into the park and had the place almost to ourselves, except for moose, red squirrels and chipmunks, as we climbed through the remnants of the winter's snow and ice.

The New England winters were particularly novel for me. Coming as I did from the mild climate of Melbourne where if it snowed at all it was just a dusting and rated a front page picture in the daily paper, I was not used to temperatures that fell below freezing for days on end, or snow falling so hard that a meter of it could accumulate in just a few hours.

One morning I got out of bed at 6 a.m., when it was still dark, dressed and had breakfast, then opened the back door to go to work. In front of me was a waist-high wall of snow where the black bitumen of our drive had been the night before. I stood, astounded, then turned and went back inside barely able to believe so much snow could fall in one night. Listening to the news later in the morning we heard that the governor had declared a state-of-emergency and closed all roads in the area. It was one of the heaviest falls on record.

In late 1978 my mother was diagnosed with cancer. In April of the following year we decided to move back to Australia to be nearer to her. We found a house in East Malvern, close to many of my family and friends, and I returned to working for my father's engineering company.

After many periods in the hospital my mother came home in intense pain. There was nothing more the doctors could do for her except prescribe a narcotic pain killer called a Brompton's Cocktail. This gave her some peace but at the very end I don't think even this helped. At one point she told me she wanted to die a Catholic. She wanted to be converted because, she said, "They believe in a life after death." She asked me if she should, and I gave her a flippant answer, as I did to all her important questions.

During her last hours, when I went up to her room, I heard her dying, heard her last breathe, the rasping gurgle in her throat. At the very end each of us paraded up one by one to say our private goodbyes. I remember going up and sitting beside her. Her face was creamy white, her eyes stared up at the ceiling and her silver-gray hair was spread out on the pillow. I talked to her, but if she could hear me, I don't know. I wanted to say so many things but stupidly I thought that being a man precluded me from intimacy, even with my mother. During her last hours we all sat around the dining room table waiting. I don't remember if it was sunny or raining. I didn't cry, I didn't mourn. I went through the motions. I did what I felt was expected but I didn't have the words, the feelings.

On the day of her death I didn't comprehend that I would never speak to her again. There was a nurse in the house and her doctor. He was more emotional about it all than I was. I was physically there in her room, but I wasn't there in my head. I sat downstairs drinking and making small talk with the family, not admitting to myself what was happening. A stiff upper lip was what I thought I had to have.

I deeply regret that I never found the courage to talk to my mother about my transgenderism but it was all part of the pattern I had developed to protect myself. I had walled myself off from those around me when I was very young and had become accomplished at rebuffing any form of contact that threatened to reveal who I really was. I was so scared that someone would guess how I felt that I shut myself off totally from close emotional contact with everyone, even Laurie and my mother. My theory was that if I maintained a wall around myself and let no one in, then no one would ever get close enough to discover my horrible secret.

After she died my mother's jewelry was divided among my sisters and Laurie. I sat at the table and watched as they chose various items. I wanted so much to have some of those beautiful remembrances but it was not possible. They had meant a lot to her and it was not the monetary value I missed but the intrinsic value to me. She had left them to the women of the family and I was not one of them.

Years later I found a small hand-made silver 'J' on a silver chain that was hers. It is a precious possession.

Chapter Five

In the years following my mother's death Laurie and I had a lot of happy times traveling around the country, camping in the Australian bush and sharing the experiences we both loved so much. We bought an old Land Rover and explored the coastal region of eastern Victoria, the High Plains and the Victorian Alps, up into the northwest desert country of Wyperfeld National Park and the Kulkyne Forest along the Murray River.

We were both avid bird watchers and Laurie had written her college thesis on the status of the Night Parrot, believed by many at the time to be extinct. I was chairperson of the Conservation Committee of the Bird Observers Club of Victoria and during my time on the committee Laurie and I took many trips to search for Plains Wanderers, a type of quail believed to be rare in Western Victoria, to Gippsland to look for Grass Parrots and to the Wimmera in the North-West to photograph an unusual influx of Bustards to the area. We coordinated the collection of information and helped prepare the clubs submissions to the Land Conservation Council of Victoria, a state government body that at the time was doing a comprehensive survey of the flora, fauna and land use for the state.

We spent time at two of our favorite spots. One was the Hattah Lakes/Kulkyne region along the Murray River. Here it was possible to drive out into the sand dunes and billabongs and camp beneath old River Red Gums. Each morning as the sun rose the birds and animals would come from the surrounding arid country to drink. Major Mitchell Cockatoos would call from the trees as they arched their heads forward and exposed the vibrant peach and pink hues in their crest to the morning sun. Doves called incessantly in low notes that almost blended into the background noise of the bush so the only time you really noticed their song was when it stopped, or they flew off suddenly on whirring wings. Emus would strut into the waterholes making their strange grunting calls as they came. Disturbed, they ran stiff-legged, their coarse, gray feathers rising and falling like short, multi-layered tulle skirts.

Australia, unlike most countries, has few dangerous animals so camping is relatively safe. The animals that are dangerous are mainly the ones that have gone feral after escaping from the farms of the early settlers such as pigs and buffalo. One day while walking through the trees to watch parrots near Lake Hattah we heard what we believed to be wild pigs, which we knew could be extremely dangerous, coming toward us. There were lots of grunts and sounds of large animals approaching noisily but invisibly through the scrub. We looked at each other and whispered plans of how we might escape what we were sure was a family of wild pigs. In our minds they were being led by a massive old boar with curling white tusks and the temper of a mad bull.

Alone, maybe thirty kilometers from the nearest medical help, we looked around for a tree to climb, but none were big enough. Our only option was to run for the car, about a kilometer away, and we were about to start when we saw a flock of five emus striding toward us grunting and coughing in their strange voices. We stood stock still, surprised and relieved, as we watched these prehistoric-looking birds slowly pass by us a few meters away in the scrub.

Our other favorite spot was Wonboyn Lake on the south coast of New South Wales, near the Victoria border. We spent many days there fishing, swimming and bird watching. Sometimes we went with a group of friends but on many occasions it was just the two of us, looking for the beautiful green and white Wompoo Pigeons, or just sitting on the verandah watching the Spine-tailed Swifts as they dove and twisted at incredible speeds, wind whistling through their wings, before turning and spiraling back up toward the clouds and out of sight. Often on days that we saw the Swifts there would be a thunder storm. We sat in silence as the rain thundered on the corrugated iron roof and beat holes in the surface of the lake, the skies lighting up over hills to the south with bolts of lightning that formed a continuous lattice between sky and land for hours on end.

Our mutual love for nature, and particularly the Australian bush, seemed to suppress any stress between us and my gender dysphoria faded for a while, into the background of our lives.

We could both sit awed by the sight of natural beauty with little need for talk. In the evening we read or listened to music and then quietly wandered off to bed. We spent very few weekends at home over the years, preferring to go into the bush or down to an ocean beach and walk.

Throughout our marriage we supplemented our income by buying older houses, renovating them, then selling them a year or two later for a profit. The first house we owned was a single

fronted row house in Port Melbourne. This was followed by an old farm house in Shelton, Connecticut, and then half of a subdivided Victorian house in East Malvern. We worked well together on these projects, sharing the work load and combining our varied skills at wallpapering, painting and carpentry.

When they were around, Laurie's parents helped. The times when they were with us were the closest I felt to being a part of a family. I felt closer to Fred and Marje, Laurie's parents, than to my father. Fred and I did things together like sailing and working on our houses that my own father and I never had. My father was always there for his children if we got into some type of trouble, but never if we just needed a friend to sit and talk to or go fishing with.

Laurie and I worked on our house in East Malvern and then sold it and moved to a small apple orchard in Officer, just to the east of Melbourne. Here we had room for Laurie to have horses, and for me to have chickens. We made new friends and soon adopted a wonderful son, Sam.

We had always thought of adopting a child as well as giving birth to our own. After many attempts during which the pregnancy never went full term, we gave up and started adoption proceedings instead. Whether the failure was in the sperm or the egg I do not know, but I have never regretted not being able to 'father' a son. It is not in my nature to feel that a child by intercourse is any more a part of the family than an adopted one.

Going through the process of adopting we were asked if we wanted a boy or a girl. Our reply was that in natural birth one is not given that option so we would not presume to take it when adopting—we would accept the first child available to us, irrespective of sex.

After a year of formalities—interviews and government paperwork—we were approved by the state agency for an inter-country adoption. The normal procedure was to forward our file to the country of our choice and then wait to be advised if we were or were not acceptable to them. If acceptable we would then go over and select a child, and bring the child back with us. The procedure could take up to six months.

What happened, instead, was that we got a call one afternoon to come into the city office before five. I left work and Laurie drove in from home, about forty-five minutes away and we got there at five o'clock. We were ushered into an office and told that there was a child available for adoption in Melbourne and did we want to see him. We jumped at the opportunity. The next morning at the foster care home we were introduced to Sam by the woman who had been looking after him. He was three months old. We held him while the other children played around us.

"When can we take him home," I asked, expecting it would be in a week or two.

"Oh not until tomorrow," she said. "My husband likes to say goodbye to all the children before they leave."

That gave us one day to buy and borrow everything from bottles and nappies to prams and cots. I called my sister Mandy, and asked her if she could bring over some things she had and I took the day off work so we could go shopping to set up the house. We picked Sam up just thirty-six hours after we were told he was available.

I have often wondered whether or not I should have gone through with the adoption, but at the time I still thought that I had some control over where I was going. I still thought I could control my desires and needs and be a father forever.

To the outside world we were the perfect family, and in most ways we were. Sam grew and changed and showed us both a new level of pleasure as he explored his life with us. He came on all the camping trips, though they were less frequent. Around the farm he learn how to swim, pick apples and collect eggs.

We soon found he was strong-willed too and would not tolerate something he did not like. We tried confining him in a play pen once or twice but his screamed objections were so loud that we gave up and let him have the run of the house.

We all enjoyed so many common interests that every day and every trip could be shared closely. There was only one topic that Laurie and I ever really fought about in all our years of marriage. And it hung over us like a dead weight.

About a year after we moved to the orchard the family engineering company that I was working for failed, due to an economic recession and the loss of some key employees. At the time I was struggling hard with my gender dysphoria and was sure that the loss was entirely my fault, despite the fact that many other small companies were also folding.

I had put nearly all the money we had, about $40,000, into the company and this was now gone. All we had left was our equity in the orchard and a small amount of savings. I was soon to be unemployed and had no qualifications other than my years of experience. My self esteem fell and I was close to a total breakdown. I stayed at the office alone at night, crying and yelling at the walls for hour upon hour, worrying about what was to become of my life and marriage and finding no solution to the problem. I wandered around the empty office recounting figures and looking at books trying to work out how we were to survive. Finally I came to the conclusion that there was nothing to do but get on with life as best I could.

Since I was now unemployed, we decided to try and make a living from growing apples. We borrowed some money from Laurie's father and together we took on the task of looking after the one thousand apple trees. I also worked as a casual picker and in the packing sheds of nearby orchards. The first year we ran the orchard we lost money because we had not thinned the apples hard enough. The second we lost more, because there was a drought and we did not have enough dams on the property to water the trees. Then, in 1985, we were in the path of the Ash Wednesday bush fires.

I had never been near a bush fire before and did not know what was coming. The first we knew about it was seeing a small column of smoke on the horizon way off in the west. We talked to the neighbors and listened to the radio and came to the conclusion that the fires were too far from us to worry about. This was at about ten in the morning. By eleven the smoke was looking much closer and, listening to the news, we realized that not only was the fire coming our way, it was coming very fast. What was originally a calm report from a news reader had become a series of news flashes interrupting normal broadcasting and read excitedly. We were told that the fire was large and out of control. We should be ready to evacuate immediately.

We loaded up the car with all our valuables and pointed it out the drive. We then opened the gates in the boundary fence into our neighbor's property and chased the horses through, further from the approaching smoke and fire. The only other thing that could be done then was to fill the tractor with diesel fuel and

65

the one thousand liter orchard sprayer with water, and wait, which is what we did.

We did not want Sam to be so close to the danger so we put him in his carry basket and drove him to a neighbor's house, further from the approaching flames, then returned to try and save our house and orchard.

News reports by now had the fire about ten kilometers from us and we started to see fire trucks going past our gate and up the hill toward it. Soon the smoke was high overhead and the sun turned a bright rust color. The smoke was so thick that it did not hurt our eyes to look up at the sun, and as the fire got closer the smoke came lower and we could see no more than a few hundred meters in any direction. The smell of burning was intense and ash began raining down on us as we made what final preparations we could.

The horses had panicked and returned to their stalls and, despite our frantic efforts, we could not get them out again so we resigned ourselves to the fact that they would just have to fend for themselves. We felt totally helpless.

The fire was now on the other side of the hill from us, according to what we heard from reports on the radio and from friends who lived in that direction. We could see flames. Cars loaded with people and their belongings were coming down our road away from the fire and more trucks were speeding toward it loaded with volunteer fire fighters. We realized our feeble little orchard sprayer would not even be able to slow the fire down, let alone stop it.

The horses were out of control and we were alone with only a few paddocks of dry grass between us and a wall of fire. Laurie and I just sat together in the dirt of our drive watching and waiting. The roar from the flames was now so loud that it was hard to even talk. We just sat, covered in ash and dust with our eyes watering, and waited for the fire to come to us.

Despite all this I was still feeling quite calm. I had no idea what to expect and was naive to the magnitude of our danger. Occasionally I drove the tractor up into the next orchard to see what was happening, and then back to wait again with Laurie. Fire trucks were racing up and down the road and water tankers were stopping and refilling from our dam beside the road.

The heat around us was intense because, not only had the day been hot, but we could now feel the flames as they came down the hill toward us. The fire had reached our boundary fence.

By now I knew there was nothing we could do to stop its advance and was resigned to the fact that we would lose every-thing—animals, orchard, house and possessions. It was time to get Sam and drive away, leaving it to luck and the firefighters to do their best.

But the wind that had been gradually dying down finally stopped. The advance of the fire slowed. We thought perhaps there was still a chance. Suddenly with a roar the winds strength-ened again, harder than before, but this time from the south, behind us, fresh and strong. Leaves and ash swirled back toward the fire and it took off with renewed vigor parallel to our bound-ary, but away. We were saved, but many more of our neighbors, and their neighbors for many kilometers beyond them, were now in the peril we had just escaped.

With the new wind direction the sky above us cleared and it was possible to watch the front of the fire race along the crest of the hill in front of us. Balls of flame jumped ahead of the main fire, appearing to roll with a life of their own across the tree tops, igniting them as they went. The fire was going so fast that with-in five minutes it was no longer visible, and there was an eerie silence all around, broken only by the occasional truck carrying fire fighters coming back past our house, trying to catch up with the fire.

I took the tractor with its spray unit out and did what little I could to help extinguish the hot-spots in burnt out tree trunks and other places in our adjoining bushland. We then started to hear that some of our neighbors, further up the road, had died.

One family perished when they had returned home to look for their father and had become trapped. He had already left and was safe. We were told they had died from suffocation as the fire sucked the oxygen from the air around them, before it burnt their bodies to ash.

All but a lucky few people had lost everything in the flames yet strangely, every now and then in the middle of this devastated landscape, there would be one home left totally unscathed, surrounded by nothing but blackened dirt and smoldering trees.

The fire had been so intense that there wasn't even any ash left on the ground. It had all been blown away by the wind that had been generated within the fire by the speed of its own advance.

The day after the fire the first car loads of sightseers came past, slowly, occupants peering out of the windows and pointing. It seemed gruesome and macabre that strangers would want to come and see where our friends had lost everything, and where people we had known had died. We felt like screaming at them to leave us alone, to be more respectful of the suffering of others.

For days afterwards, the slightest breeze would have us going out to watch for fresh outbreaks. We regularly woke in the middle of the night sure we could smell smoke and, if the wind came hot and dry from the north, we would immediately fill the spray unit with water, just in case. Even now, years later, the smell of burning leaves or a hot dry wind is enough to reawaken the memories.

All my life I had been ambivalent about sex, and our marriage quickly became almost celibate—a situation that I realize now was extremely hard and unfair on Laurie. I loved being married to her but I wanted to be able to have sex as a woman, to have sex as a lesbian. The strain on our marriage was becoming unbearable. I didn't want to break up the family but I did want to be recognized as a woman.

By this time, early 1983, I was buying my own dresses and I knew that I had to find some professional help somewhere. I realized I would have to go to a friend or stranger and ask for help. It was late 1984 before I actually gave up rationalizing why

I should not start, and finally made a contact.

The act of searching for help was soul destroying. I was exposing my innermost emotions and secrets to complete strangers and had no idea what their reaction would be. It was only when I reached the bottom of my despair and had lost all self-esteem that I could finally bring myself to make those calls. I felt as though I was calling up and saying, "I am a pervert of no worth, is there anything that I can do?" Worst of all, it took many calls before I found help.

Again and again I exposed myself to dispassionate voices at the end of the phone line. And every time I went into all the details, gave as full an explanation of what a transsexual was as I could, mostly they had no idea what I was asking about. They had not heard the word transsexual or, if they had, they had only the barest idea of what it meant. The blankness in their voices almost made me give up but I knew that unless I persevered Laurie would take Sam and go.

I knew very little about transexualism at this point myself. I knew the word and I knew it was the medical definition for how I felt but I could not explain all of its ramifications. My main aim was to find counseling and try and find out for myself what my options were. I did not approach this search for information as a way to 'cure' my need to be accepted as a woman. It was a search for knowledge and direction on how I was going to live my life as a woman. I wanted to know how to become accepted, what I had to do to live openly as a woman. Over the years I had heard of people like Christine Jorgenson so I knew that the possibility existed, what I did not know was how much I would have to give up to achieve my dream. That was what I had to find out.

It was just as hard for Laurie to live through this time, prob-ably harder, as it was beyond her control. All she could do was insist that I get help and then wait for the outcome. We would spend many nights and days in strained semi-silence as I made the calls and kept appointments, searching for an answer.

My first contact was with a family friend who had done some 'life-line' work. Laurie and I went together and told her the whole story. She said that she did not know of any transsexuals, but she gave us the number of a government department that might be able to help. It took three calls before I found the right department. They said they couldn't help but to try a clinic they had heard of. One more call and this time the receptionist said they had a psychologist on staff who did some work with trans-sexuals.

The clinic was helpful but, for me, who had no idea what to expect, they pushed faster than I was ready to go. I sat and told the doctor everything—what I wanted and all the smallest details of my family life and upbringing. Over the next few months I wrote long essays for him detailing my emotions and fantasies. It was a great help for me to openly examine my feelings and for the first time I was honest enough to say to another person that I was not looking for a cure, I wanted to be a woman. The relief of actually talking to someone about the problem was invigorating and for awhile I took a new interest in life and the day-to-day chores and problems seemed to dissolve before me.

I never spoke to Laurie about all the details of my visits. It would have been too threatening for me and our relationship. I kept all my discussions very general and positive in the hope that I could come to some resolution for myself and eventually life would go on smoothly forever.

The psychologist finished evaluating me and after about three months was prepared to start me on hormones and begin my transition immediately. He gave me a referral to an endocri-nologist at Royal Women's Hospital—and I panicked. I was going to become a woman, with breasts and everything I had ever wanted; but I wasn't ready. It would mean the end of my marriage. The loss of Sam. The scorn of my friends. I did not keep the appointment and never went back to the psychologist. I returned to trying to fight the problem on my own. This was a mistake and I steadily reverted to my old habits.

Soon after I stopped visiting the clinic, in September 1985, we had another major disaster. The orchard was hit by a hail storm and our whole year's income was lost in ten minutes. All the fruit on the trees had grown to about the size of golf balls and the hail tore or bruised the majority of them. We were at the very start of the storm's trail of destruction and further down its path it intensified. The orchards belonging to some of our friends had the leaves and fruit literally torn from the trees.

I walked dazed down the rows of carefully tended apple trees, picking a small fruit here, turning another in my fingers there. Ninety percent of the crop was ruined. Our year's income was gone as were most of our financial resources. We were left with the option of trying to sell the fruit for juice-making, or selling the orchard and cutting our losses.

Then, the large trustee company where we had the last of our cash reserves, five thousand dollars, went bankrupt and we lost it all.

In the space of five years, my mother had died, the family engineering company had failed, we had suffered bushfires, drought and hail storms, I had started counseling—and stopped it—and we were just about out of money. We were not the orchard owners worst affected by the storm but it was the last straw. I gave up.

Our marriage and relationship was also strained to breaking by the combination of events. We both saw the probability that we would divorce fairly soon and felt that there would be more support for Laurie and Sam from her family, rather than from mine. So we put the orchard on the market and started making plans to move, for the second time, back to New England.

Our idea was that I would stay in America for six months or so, until Laurie and Sam were settled, and then return to Melbourne alone. I had no plan at all beyond that. It seemed our marriage was finally at an end. Yet despite everything I still felt I could cure my desire to be a woman if I tried hard enough.

The orchard finally sold in April 1986 and, after paying off all our loans,we had a small amount of money. In May we packed what was left of our personal belongings, including our German Short-haired Pointer, Annie, and flew to Vermont.

Chapter Six

In going to Vermont I was running away from my past. I wanted to leave 'Jennifer' in Australia and start again. Maybe Laurie and I would not need to divorce after all. I was still grasping for an ever diminishing thread. Before leaving I collected all my women's clothes, which I had hidden all over the house, put them in a bag, and threw them into the rubbish. I felt that this new start would save me. Never again would I need to wear a dress.

But there was one pair of new pantyhose, still in their packet, that I could not part with. It seemed such a waste. I put them in the case with the rest of my clothes.

How I could have, for one moment, seriously thought that anything would change, I do not know. My recognition of who I really was was so strong, yet the desire to remain a part of the family was, at the time, even stronger. I was bound to both my family and my femininity, and they were drifting inexorably apart. Yet even though I felt the pain I did not see the only possible outcome. I still did not realize I could not have both.

Laurie's parents lived near Hanover, New Hampshire, so we found a house to rent in nearby Thetford, Vermont. Within six months of moving I turned around, and there was 'Jennifer.' I welcomed her with open arms and the old patterns returned. I went down to the local mall and bought some underwear and stockings and hid them in a draw. With these new clothes, the fights and tears began again. The Salvation Army benefited from my remorse and over the next year or two more dresses and

72

clothes were given away and more money lost.

When we first arrived in Vermont we both found work on a local market-garden farm while I started looking for more permanent work. The change from Australia to America relieved some of the stress on our marriage and I remained beyond the original plan of six months. I applied for a job designing super-insulated homes, despite the fact that I had never done this type of work before. I told them that I knew all about it and they said I could start. My theory was that I had done some engineering drawing, I knew some basic geometry from school and I knew what I liked in a house, therefore it would be no problem for me to join these skills and do the job. As it turned out my theory worked and it only took a small amount of bluff in the initial stages to get me through. Once I knew how the company worked all I had to do was talk to the clients and get their ideas, then transfer the ideas onto paper. I really enjoyed the job and the people I worked with, and it was satisfying to see my ideas develop from drawings to finished houses and satisfied owners.

I worked for about a year until the company went bankrupt, then applied for, and got, the job as manager of a local builders' supply company. I worked there until 1990 when it was taken over and my job was given to the brother of the new owner.

We had left Australia in May of 1986 and from then until May of 1987 I made no attempt to look for help. In May 1987 Laurie and I had a major fight over my transgenderism. Laurie's patience with my 'cross-dressing' was wearing out. She had tolerated it for over ten years and was now venting her anger and frustration. This time she did it more strongly and loudly than ever before, and it had a more marked effect on me than ever before.

I felt now that the end of the marriage really was just a matter of time, so I decided that I had to start to do something for myself. I wasn't ready to seek professional help again, but I started a diary so that I could keep track of myself and see if I could learn something.

I had never looked at myself closely before except that one time in Australia. Denial works best if you don't examine the source of your angst too closely, so throughout my life I had kept well away from too many questions. Emotionally I was a disaster and I always had been. All my life I had tried to prove I was a man and to help do this I repressed my emotional expression. I had ended up convincing everyone of my manliness except myself.

I started to write things down and think about them. The next step, I decided, would be for me to seek out professional help again. I had found help in Australia so at least I knew I could do it when the time came. It would just be, once more, a case of picking up the phone, taking a few deep breaths and calling around until I found someone.

I had a lot to learn but the one thing I knew for sure was, if Laurie and I did part, as it seemed we surely would one day, I would not be looking for a man to become my partner. My lesbianism was one of the strongest things holding me to the marriage. I loved Laurie, and she was also my closest friend. I had no personal need to leave. There was nothing to give me the impetus for that final step out of our marriage; certainly no craving for male sexual contact.

Even the stress related to my gender dysphoria was bearable because I had lived with it all my life. I knew no other emotional level. There was nothing that I could look back to and compare my current situation with. There was no bench mark I could strive to return to. In all its apparent abnormality my life and what I was living through was, to me, normal.

By degrees, my gender dysphoria was demanding more of my time and mental energy now. I was demanding more from those around me. But it had been that way before and had subsided, so I expected it to do so again. I hoped life would revert to what I was used to and all would continue as 'normal.'

Beginning a diary marked the start of my long trip out of the closet. I decided the next step was to find the strength within me to talk to Laurie's parents and to try and explain to them why I did what I did. I would no longer pretend they didn't know. I decided I might as well get things out in the open. For the first time I also started some searching conversations with Laurie and we began seriously confronting our mutual problem. My denial was starting to fall away and I was beginning to test the reaction I got from people when I spoke to them about my gender dysphoria. Starting the diary was like turning on a tap and although there were hesitations along the way the first drips of coming out soon grew to a steady, unstoppable stream.

Although Laurie had told her parents about the nature of our problem, soon after the fight Laurie and I had in May I decided to come out to her mother. She did not desert me, but she did try and convince me that I should change my ways and stay the man that she thought she knew. I was desperate to find an ally and at the time I thought, naively, that she might support me in my desire to live as a woman. I soon found that this was not the case.

It was hard to come to terms with the fact that my new found confidante had her daughter's best interests at heart and that she did not want to see a transgendered person as part of her daughter's life, no matter how she felt about me personally. I began to learn that I had to moderate my excitement and slow down. I could sense that as I expressed my joy at my coming out she, and later others, backed away. She could not share my joy.

On the 4th of June 1987 I found the strength to sit down with Laurie's father and tell him. The mental energy and strength required to tell anyone was enormous, but he was the hardest for me. I had known him for twenty-five years, longer than I had known Laurie. We had sailed over fifteen thousand miles together and had gone through incredible life threatening experiences, and had shared many beautiful ones as well. He was more of a role model to me than my father. He already knew about me from Laurie and Marje but I had to come out to him myself. I had to risk losing one of the most important people in my life.

I told him and again there was a level of acceptance. He expressed no pleasure at sharing my joy of growing, but I wonder now why I had expected it. I was destroying a balance, a way of life, security. It was all going up in flames. Why did I expect other people to share my happiness?

One thing I learned during this period was that there is no good time to tell people. I had to pick a time, and do it. I couldn't wait for someone else to start the conversation. I had to be the one. It was as hard for them as it was for me, often harder, because I knew a lot about gender dysphoria and they had no concept at all of what it was, or what it meant for me to live with it.

Although dialogue was now open, my personal life did not really improve. There was still the constant battle over my need for women's clothes. I was now wearing women's underwear fairly continually and it hurt Laurie to see or know it. She tolerated it for some months but I was still lying to both myself and others. I was still denying to myself that I was a woman and that I wanted to have a sex change.

Even so, in my diary entries I wrote that I could contain my need to be seen and accepted as a woman indefinitely, yet this need for acceptance and for being seen as a woman was incredibly strong and growing despite my written and verbal protestations. I desperately wanted someone to look at me and say, "Yes I can see you are a woman." I was crying out for it with my every action and word. The life I had known was slowly crumbling around me, but I did not truly want to stop and save that life, for it would have meant abandoning my womanhood.

By the end of 1987 I was finally admitting to myself that, at the very least, I would never stop needing some form of outward female expression in my life.

The struggle between Laurie and I continued in the background, yet I did not have the courage to sit down with her and discuss our future together. The risk of her leaving me was still too great. Just talking was not easy for me. We would go to bed and I would lie there in the dark, working out in my head how I was to open the conversation. I would concoct long conversations, planning over and over again what I would say, then what

Laurie would answer, and how in turn I would answer that. Usually by the time I plucked up the courage to speak I felt it was too late in the night, so I would just go to sleep vowing that the next day I would use the words I had found. The next day normally found me rationalizing why the time was still not quite right. But the time is never right. I would just have to start.

The turmoil through those years was draining. I continued lying, twisting meanings, rationalizing actions and doing all I could to be a woman and at the same time stay a man.

By April 1988 I was hanging dresses in my closet where Laurie, and anyone else, could see them. I had just about pushed her tolerance too far. When alone, I wore dresses most of the time and I had given up using men's underwear totally.

The closet door was open and I was stepping out. I started walking through the woods in a dress to see my father-in-law whenever we were both home alone. He tolerated me in a dress but it must have been very hard for him and I owe him a lot for his tolerance. The walk was about half a kilometer through dense Vermont pine and spruce forest on his land, as our blocks abutted, so I felt reasonably safe that I would not be detected.

My need to be seen as a woman had become obsessive and I had little regard or consideration left for the feelings of others. I was pushing the acceptable boundaries hard and I enjoyed being able to move about with some degree of freedom. For some reason I did not see the pain I was causing my family and was blind to the fact that I could not go on this way forever.

The open display of clothes in the closet finally brought things to a head. Laurie confronted me again and there was another fight, this time with serious threats of divorce, and my banishment from the family. The thrust this time was "what about our son?" He was seven and becoming more observant. What damage would it do? What if he saw me? I pleaded that I would be careful. What if someone else found out about me? The scandal would be terrible. We would have to leave town. The clothes had to go if I was going to stay. More tears and again a promise from me of "never again."

This time however I did not get rid of all my women's clothes. I kept most of them, hidden in a box in the attic and at the back of one of my drawers, and in the closet. I was back to wearing only underwear and even Laurie did not know. Again I had to control my physical contact with her, her hand could not even touch my bottom in case she felt that slide of pantyhose on nylon underwear. Again I was lying.

The continual need to lie is awful and it put a huge stress on me and, consequently, on my relations with Laurie. I lied about my true feelings. I lied about wearing women's clothes. I lied just by trying to carry on the pretense of being male. My whole life was a lie and I hated it.

And yet other aspects of my life were wonderful. I had a great family and we went skiing, fishing and hiking together. When we could forget the shadow of my secret we were very happy. Laurie and I had been married for fourteen years. We were good friends and shared many common interests. Neither of us wanted the marriage to end. Then, one sunny day in June 1988 the end came. I finally 'disgraced' the family in front of friends.

I had reached a point where I could no longer tolerate having to stay in the closet and was again pushing very hard at the limits of my family's tolerance by taking less care about what I wore and how I hid my illicit wardrobe of clothing. It was as though, subconsciously, I wanted to create a confrontation that would prove to my family that I was a woman. I should have known that such an occurrence would be a disaster. I did not knowingly see or avoid it though and started taking less and less care about being caught. I was desperate for approval. I took more and greater risks. At about 11 p.m. one night Sam and I were alone in the house. I was getting ready for bed and, thinking Sam would be well asleep, decided to try on a dress, just for a minute or two. I had just finished putting it on when I heard Sam behind me and turned around. He looked at me and asked what I was doing. I gave him some weak excuse and sent him back to bed with a promise I would be down in a moment to tuck him in. I put on my pajamas, went down and gave him a kiss and hoped that he wouldn't say anything to anyone later. I knew the chances were slim since I did not tell him not to say anything or even speak sternly to him about it. I did not want to start him on a path of lying for me. I knew the story would probably come out of him at some time and I was prepared to accept the consequences, but I did not guess how bad the timing of his disclosure would be. Some days later at a sunny summer lunch on the front deck, he light-heartedly told the whole family, including some family friends from Australia who were visiting, what he had seen.

The result was instant and catastrophic. Laurie left in tears, followed by her mother, while I just sat and tried to brazen it out. Later, for the first time ever, Laurie screamed at me and I stood and took it all. These were not just tears or silent recriminations as in the past. This was a violent outburst. I knew that I had caused irreparable hurt to everyone involved. I found out later how much I had hurt Laurie when we tried to talk about what had happened. We were in the kitchen doing the dishes when her anger and frustration reached the point that she threw down a knife which landed, quivering, with its point in the floor. This was the only time in our long relationship that there had been any type of violent physical outburst between us.

The next day I was standing beside the road waiting to be picked up from work. Loaded sand trucks were coming past and I knew they could not stop in a hurry. All I had to do was take two quick steps forward onto the road. I didn't do it because of the anguish it would have caused the driver, but I am glad that I did not own a gun at that time. A day or two later I sat on the top of a cliff and considered again the possibility of taking my life. I looked down and saw dead branches and rocks below me, littered around the base of the majestic trees whose heads rose above me. If I had stood up and stepped forward I could have joined those tree-limbs twenty meters below me. I would not have had to worry any more about being a transgendered lesbian. I sat for more than an hour considering all my options and possible life choices and finally came to terms with the fact that the most important thing in my life was to one day become a woman and live openly that way.

That was not the first time I had considered taking my life, nor the last, but it was the closest I ever came to actually doing it.

The shock of that horrific lunch was too much for my earlier resolve. I was deeply ashamed and did not want to bring any more pain to Laurie or her family. Yet at the same time I realized I could not suppress my gender dysphoria completely. Once more I promised that I would never cross-dress again. I returned to pretending I was a normal male. I returned to the closet and stayed firmly locked in it until June 1989.

Although the resolve to stay closeted had initially been strong it steadily weakened until it reached the point that Laurie knew that I was again wearing women's clothes, and this time we sat and talked.

Those June 1989 discussions with Laurie were the first time I was prepared to admit to myself that I could no longer drift along, that I had to finally acknowledge to myself, once and for-ever, that I would never change. I would always need to express my true feelings and emotions.

The reason it took me so long to get to this stage of talking openly to Laurie was the fear that if I told her that I really want-ed to live the rest of my life as a woman she would leave me and I would lose everything that I had ever worked for. I believed at this time that I was being totally honest when I told her I could live happily if I were just allowed to cross-dress openly within the house, but in reality I was still holding back. Subconsciously I knew, though I could not yet admit openly to her or to myself, that my life-long dream was for hormones, surgery and a com-plete sex change and I was not going to stop until I got it.

The incredible shame and guilt I felt in being transgendered was not because of how I felt about my gender, but because of the impact I was having on those I loved. When I was five I sensed that I had a secret that I could not share. When I turned twelve this knowledge was certain. From my earliest memories I knew that what I wanted most in life was frowned upon by those around me. Initially I did not know why, I just hid and listened, slowly learning words like 'queer' and 'perverted.' I was still too young to know what those words meant, I just knew they were not good, and that they applied to me. As I got older I became defensive. I was sure that I was not evil, and yet there was that shadow of doubt. What if I really was evil? I kept hiding the things I thought and did and slowly learned more. I found that what people call cross-dressing was seen as a sin.

In my teens I resolved to change and conform to society's rules, then I found that I could not do it. I had failed and my guilt deepened. I grew older and did not seem to get the same pleasure from the opposite sex that my friends did. I reasoned that I must be homosexual, and the guilt grew larger. I tried to prove my male gender to myself and others, but inside I knew that it was not working. By my every action I was lying to myself and those around me. I was prepared to say or do anything to hide my feminine side. I was failing again and this confirmed to me that I had very little self-worth. And so the spiral of learning guilt continued.

I had now learned, at the age of forty-three, that I was sick of the shame and lying. I went searching for the truth.

We were living near Dartmouth College so I used their library to find out what other people were doing about their transgenderism. I started by finding books and reading as much as I could. Was I a perverted person or was it something more? The search was long and lonely.

I found out some things that I wished were not true; some in the medical profession were advocating counseling and other treatments as a way of curing what they saw to be a psychiatric illness. I found out some things that I was glad about; many other people had gone through what I was going through and had ended up leading productive lives. For all the negatives I turned up it was still enlightening and a true awakening. But it was also a very stressful time. Every now and again I lost my composure and wanted to scream, "I am not a freak. I am not a pervert. I am not a threat. I am a woman, a lesbian!"

I became obsessed with my studying. I spent hours in the library and many more absorbed in my own thoughts. Laurie and her family tried hard to stand by me and, for most of the time, they did. It would have been immeasurably harder without them. I was taking someone they knew, and was slowly and inexorably replacing that person with one who was visibly different, and they didn't know how to react to the change. I loved them and I hoped and prayed that they could learn to like the new me.

Our financial stress increased too as I was not working much, and certainly was not looking for any permanent or high-paying work. To live from day to day we were eating into our savings. Fortunately these had been replenished since we left Australia by the selling of a family company and the distribution of most of its capital.

Throughout this time I was scared and lonely. No one else shared my enthusiasm for what I was learning. I sometimes wondered if I should give up and yet I knew that I could not, nor did I want to. I was in the early stages of transition and had a long way to go.

During those early transitional months I read every book and professional journal I could find on transgenderism and took a part-time job on the same local market-garden farm that I had worked on when we arrived. This allowed me the time I needed to go to the library and consume large quantities of the pros and cons of transgenderism. I read Stoller who said I wasn't crazy, and other works that said I was. I read that a good shot of electricity would cure me and show that my actions and reactions to transgenderism were purely due to conditioning and that I could be electrically 'de-conditioned.'

My learning was almost like a binge-drinking session, where I sat and consumed everything, but did not fully understand all of it. It was only when the initial rush was over and I calmed down that I could go back and re-read the literature in a more detached fashion. Perhaps that first reading was just for me to know that other people were transgendered and that people were writing books that said I was not crazy.

I was like a mare that had bolted for home and there was no stopping me. Even if someone had offered me a pill to take that would have let me become a man I would not have swallowed it, I had waited too long to be allowed to live as a woman. In my search I was not looking to be dissuaded from my decision to change. I was looking for permission.

Chapter Seven

The beginning of my search for a solution to being transgendered was in the stacks in the medical school at Dartmouth College. I went in, hoping that non-students were allowed to use the library and found that the only restriction was that I could not borrow books. I did not have the courage to ask for help in my search because I would have to say the word 'transgender.' Instead I taught myself how their on-line computer system worked and then wandered the floors until I found the section I needed.

I located a dozen books and some journals with references to transgenderism. I took these to a quiet desk in a corner of the stack room and sat for hours copying out pages so I could refer to them later. I would not photocopy them in case someone saw the title of the book or article I was copying. Most of what I found had been published in the late 1960s to mid-1970s and I was worried that the information was not up-to-date.

The lack of current information finally lead to the realization that there was not much written on the subject and, except for works by two or three people, nothing definitive. Authors like Green and Money were reasonably contemporary and they proved the most helpful. I devoured what was available and learned various theories. I found references to books like *Conundrum* by Jan Morris and read those. I went to the public libraries and found that, except for a few small one-line references in general sex education books, they were of no help.

My search had started. I found in those books and articles a resource that showed me that not only was I not alone, I was not even a 'perverted, sick individual.' The next step was to find a professional to help me. I was still working alone, knew no one else like me, and could not find any one. I had tried to contact some groups listed in reference books at the library, without success.

I decided it was time to find professional help again so, screwing my courage to the sticking point once more, I called the Dartmouth Medical Center and asked to talk to someone who knew something about transsexualism. Again I had exposed my soul to a stranger. Thankfully they were helpful and understanding and recommended that I see one of their psychiatrists. I made an appointment with Joel (not his real name).

Very few psychiatrists or counselors have ever worked with a transgendered person, and less have worked with one on the verge of coming out. Joel was very useful to me initially, as had been the doctor in Australia. He provided a non-judgmental ear for me to voice my feelings. He allowed me to learn more about the depth and direction of my emotions. I started by telling him I was not looking to be cured. I told him how I felt and what I wanted to achieve: I wanted to live openly as a woman as soon as I could, even if it took me years.

He listened but at each visit he suggested reasons why I should go slowly, and asked if I was sure I wanted to go forward. I ignored most of his questions and found I was using him as a sounding board for my own ideas. I voiced my fears and longings aloud and reasoned with myself as I heard my words. By the end of two months I could see that I was coming to grips with myself. I had even started to talk to Laurie and her family about my feelings without feeling abject fear and shame.

I also came to the realization that I wanted to tell all my family, including those in Australia, that I was transgendered. The American members already knew something of what I was going through but for myself I had to tell everyone personally. It was important for me to stand in front of each person and say the words. It seemed to release me from the lie I had been living.

In January 1990 I learned that my sister Sally had been diagnosed with cancer. She only had a few months to live, so I booked a ticket and returned to Australia to visit her. I decided to use this opportunity to tell my Australian family face-to-face what I was planning. I wanted everyone to know. It was as though I had found some enormous truth and I wanted to share it with everyone that mattered to me.

The visit did not go as well as I had hoped. I imagined that, having lived in the same house with me as I grew up, they would not be surprised at the truth. They all claimed, however, to have known nothing. The only person who was not totally surprised was my aunt, and all she said was that the information answered some old suspicions. In general the reception was very cool. I had hoped my family would be happy for me but they were not.

As I told people, the normal answer was "Okay, I guess I can live with it." But I see now that this was an answer based on ignorance about transgenderism. I started to realize this when my father said, after an hour discussion on the topic, "I understand. I'll support you. I'm sure everything will be all right. It's not as if you're going to be wearing a dress or something is it?"

By the time I returned to America, I had told all the immediate family. I felt I would at least be tolerated as I progressed through my change.

My mental state during the visit had been very unstable. I had become desperate to live openly as a woman and my obsessive passion obliterated every other consideration from my mind, including the fact that Sally was dying and that the family was in shock over the impending loss. This lack of consideration for what they were experiencing was compounded by the fact that, in my life-long attempt to hide and deny my true self, I had quashed all my emotional links to other people. I had erected a brick wall around myself and allowed nothing to enter. In the matter of my gender dysphoria I was totally selfish and could only see what I was going through and what I wanted. I thought that I was handling my coming-out with composure, logic and kindness, but in fact I was being irrational to the point of cruelty.

I pushed very hard at the boundaries of people's tolerance for me. While in Australia I wore a woman's nightie to bed each night and uni-sex clothing during the day. This was how I lived in America but it was odd to my Australian family. To use an old cliché, my family had shown me an inch of tolerance, and I was taking much more than a mile.

As soon as I found out that people were claiming no past knowledge of my cross-dressing and other behaviors, I should have slowed down and been more considerate; I should have given them time to become accustomed to the idea that I was transgendered.

I spent some time with Sally and she was very supportive, encouraging me to do what I felt I needed to. We had many walks around her farm together but I never asked her how she was or what she was feeling at the time about family or dying. For most of our time together I just ignored the fact of her illness thinking that it would be unkind to talk to her about it. I kept a 'stiff upper lip' and never asked about serious matters. I didn't want to intrude on her illness and yet I spoke openly of my hopes and plans. If only I had had the courage to ask if she wanted to talk to me of her emotions.

As with my mother I would now like to be able to go back and talk to her openly, though I almost feel it would not work as she had been brought up with the same values I had. She had the reputation within our family of being a strong, independent woman.

On my return to America, Laurie said that she had been thinking about our relationship and that she had decided that it was finally time for us to separate. She had had enough. She had just enjoyed a month without me and now wanted to make it permanent. She was sick of my habits and needs.

I was shattered. I had returned happy, with the mistaken belief that my Australian family understood. Now my marriage was finished. Through tears I told her that if this was the case then I was going to go ahead and start on hormones and physically become a woman.

It was the first time I had openly admitted to Laurie, or anyone other than my psychologists, that this was what I wanted. Since I had started telling people that I was transgendered I had couched my reply with "maybe" or "perhaps," always leaving myself the opportunity to refute or modify my words later.

This disclosure to Laurie was the start of a new level in our relationship. With nothing left to lose I was being totally honest about my feelings and plans, which led us for the first time to better communication and openness on the subject. The barriers were down and since I was leaving the family anyway, I spoke freely of my feelings and needs, and asked about hers. I explained to her how I had stayed away from hormones and a complete change only because I did not want to leave the family. I went through the whole story, right back to the first awakening when I was five.

Laurie said she had not realized how deeply I felt nor the length of time that I had felt that way. She thought that I just wanted to cross-dress. In the past when she had asked me if I wanted to have a sex change I had always lied with an emphatic "No." The truth was a relief. She had thought that my cross-dressing and lack of sex drive was a reflection on her. She thought it was because of her failure as a woman.

At my request, we decided to try living together a little longer, but this time as two women. I gave up all pretense of being a man with her and, within the limits of our bedroom, where my clothes were, I was a woman, and lesbian.

Mail started to arrive from Australia after my return. I realized that I had not been as well accepted as I had imagined. Most of the letters accused me of being thoughtless and cruel. One even suggested that I was suffering from a brain tumor and that I should see a specialist. Another friend suggested that if I studied a certain form of religion and saw the delusion I was living under that I could be saved by God.

The worst happened as a result of a letter I wrote back to my father. It was a very personal letter in which I went into detail about my childhood and relationships with family members. He wrote back angrily, saying that I was nothing but a 'balding, middle-aged poofter' and he had photocopied my letter and circulated it to all my friends and family. The reason, he said, was so everyone could see how crazy I was. He stated that I was no longer his child.

Soon after my return to America I went back to my psychiatrist and asked for hormones and help towards progressing on my voyage. He tried strongly to dissuade me and refused to prescribe the hormones. I kept coming to see him but felt that I was no longer progressing.

I felt that my presence was threatening to him. When I first saw him he appeared to me to be a very effeminate person with the most beautiful long copper-blonde hair I have ever seen on a man. It fell in soft, thick waves to his shoulders and was swept back in delicate curves from his face. By my third visit he had had it all cut off and had a severe short-back-and-sides cut.

He was, with my permission, recording all my visits. He also talked me into making a video in which he asked personal questions about my transgenderism and referred to me throughout as "Mr. Spry." He said at the outset that it was for a paper he was giving at a professional conference and that I was welcome to come along. He also said that I could see the finished video and edit anything I did not approve of before he presented it, and have a copy for myself if I wanted. Later, when pressed to keep his promises, he was very evasive. He withdrew his invitation for me to attend the conference and I never saw the finished video or received a copy.

Losing faith in him, I made fewer appointments. One day I called him for an appointment only to find out he had moved to a different clinic some one hundred miles away. It forced me to find a new counselor, which proved to be a fortunate thing.

Some lesbian friends recommended I approach a counselor by the name of Betty. She was very busy and tried to arrange for a colleague of hers to see me. When that wasn't possible she made room in her own schedule and agreed to work with me. I soon developed a good relationship with her and felt relaxed and confident with her ability to help me.

My home life was improving too. Now that the need to lie had been removed, Laurie and I were trying a new relationship and learning about each other. With my last pretense at being male gone I felt more relaxed talking to her and explaining my emotions. It must have been strange for her to be a party to this new relationship but I could not have been happier. I no longer had to lie about my sexuality and gender to her.

The change even gave me the strength to suggest that she develop some new interests and make friends outside the marriage. I was not a man, and our relationship was that of two very close friends who didn't have sex. She made it clear that she had no lesbian interest in me or any other woman so I felt it only fair that she should find a man to be in her life. To show her how serious I was I bought her a box of condoms and made a light-hearted yet formal presentation of them to her.

She was very interested in contra-dancing and had been going for some time without me, as after one very discouraging experience, I felt I was an absolute failure at dancing. At one dance I went to I was unsuccessfully trying to work out the intricacies of changing partners in a line dance. I became so confused that I would progress no more than one or two people before finding that my direction had changed and I had returned to an earlier partner. For the first three or four times this person was very tolerant and pointed me of in the right direction. Finally though, when I arrived in front of her again she took one look and said, with tired desperation, "Oh fuck, not you again." I dropped out of the dance and never tried again.

Laurie had made some close friends through dancing and she started seeing one man in particular. They met regularly and she often went to stay with him after a dance, while I stayed home with Sam. He also came to our place quite often and we got on very well and became good friends. I was not yet going out in public dressed as a woman so it must have been strange for him, in those first months, to be dating a married woman whose spouse said he wanted to live as a woman and was encouraging his wife to date men.

Then, in August, Laurie said it wasn't working for her and I should find somewhere else to live. I was shocked. I still had naive hopes of becoming more and more female within my family. I hoped that we could carry on with Laurie having boyfriends and me being a live-in girlfriend. I was shattered at the news from Laurie and sat crying in semi-shock until the evening closed around me.

Laurie had gone to the bedroom to be alone and I sat for some hours in the living room stewing in my thoughts. As I sat alone crying, trying to come to terms with what was happening to me, I felt the need to be totally alone. I went outside and walked to my old Alfa Spyder. I wanted to take it for a long hard drive and vent my emotions.

Violence of any form is an emotional release I have never considered. I have never wanted to hit another person, or even lash out at the family pet. There had been times when I wanted to break something but I never did it. To drive off alone was my version of screaming and throwing bottles or plates around the house. It gave me emotional release of similar intensity, but without the damage.

I tried to start the car and, as usual, it took several attempts before it would run for more than a few seconds. The engine finally caught and I waited, gunning it, until it had the power to move out of the drive. Finally it ran smoothly and I turned on the headlights. Their quartz bulbs burned a path into the night. It was a little after 10:30 pm when I reached the end of the drive and, as the rear wheels hit the road they gave a chirp as they briefly lost traction. I accelerated up the long hill and held the car in second gear until the engine was screaming and the distinctive howl of the exhaust rose to a banshee wail. I wanted to create havoc, destruction. As the engine would give no more power in second I shifted up and the rear wheels chirped again as I dropped the clutch. The car crested the hill and started down to where the bitumen changed to gravel. I was doing close to 60 mph as I hit the gravel. With the top down, the warm June night air whistled around me and a quick glance showed bright stars in a clear, dark, moonless sky.

I was driving with an emotional mixture of fear, anger and confusion, a mixture as lethal as alcohol. I did not want to die and yet, if I had, I would not have really cared.

When I got to the intersection at Mine Road I decided to take the long road down to the left, toward the small town of Norwich where I knew I could pick up the pavement again and come back to the house on sealed roads. The trees closed over the road and were lit by the beam of the headlights. I felt I was driving down a long tunnel. The poor little car hopped and skipped over the potholes as I aimed it down the narrow, twisting corridor of gravel, expending my mental turmoil on keeping it, and me, away from the tree trunks that flashed past on either side of us. Slowly my head started to clear and I began enjoying the release of the drive. The emotions of the last few hours started to subside slightly and became more focused as the brisk wind blew some of the wilder ones from my head. I reached the town and the corner that would take me back along the river road and headed north again toward home.

The ride became more even on the pavement, but still not good. Cracks and voids were left by the frosts of many long Vermont winters. I drove faster with the wind howling as I kept the car in fourth gear. I did not use fifth gear as I needed to hear the engine scream out my anguish. I needed to drive the last of my fear and emotion out through the car's exhaust pipe. I was doing 80 mph down the long straight stretch past the dairy and I hoped that the barn cats were well in bed.

I had been gone about an hour and was starting to feel better. I had cried and reasoned with myself as I slowly came to terms with what I knew I had to do. The drive had done its job of distracting me enough to allow me to sort out my deepest emotions and needs.

There was no realistic option other than to accept who I was and do something constructive about spending the remainder of my life as that person. I had to stop deceiving myself. I had to leave the marriage and live the rest of my life openly as a woman. At no point did I ever consider the option of continuing my life masquerading as a man in public and living my female self in private. I knew that even if I had to give up Laurie and Sam, I was determined to live as a woman.

Chapter Eight

Since my return from Australia Laurie had been adamant that our marriage was over and that I had to go. There had been a period of some seven months during which I had tried offering various compromise solutions, like separate beds and separate rooms, but we had reached a point where I was unwilling to give up my need to live openly as a woman, and she was no longer willing to have me in the house. Our sixteen-year marriage was finally coming to an end.

I realized that my plan to live openly as a woman would not be universally accepted, but I also knew that I was prepared to give up everything, including all my friends and family, if that was what it took. I had hit bottom at last and was ready to start over, alone if need be, but I was finally on the way to being free from the self hate and guilt of the last forty years. I started looking for a place to rent, somewhere to start my new life.

Here the Fates were looking after me. A man came into Marje's work place and, in conversation, told her that he was looking for a house to rent and had turned one down because it was too small. She got the address of the house and the name of the owner and even from the outside I knew that I would like it. It was an old one room school house. I met with the owners and learned that it was only available for the winter, but I arranged to rent it anyway. It was such a beautiful place that I would worry later about where to live the following summer. I planned to turn it into my own doll's house. I was going to have floral sheets on the bed, make-up in the bathroom, flowers in every room, and dresses in the closet.

The school house was ideal for starting a new life. There was no TV so I planned lots of classical music, reading, academic study and transgender study. I wanted it to be a learning and growing experience, one that I could come away from a new person. I wanted to move forward all the time and resolved to always be vigilant against slipping back into old ways.

My new counselor made a big difference in my ability to achieve these goals. While Joel, my first psychologist, was very helpful as a sounding board for my thoughts, I was never able to relax with him. He never asked my real name or showed an interest me. He seemed more interested in the problem rather than the patient.

With Betty, however, I was talking as a woman to a woman. She called me Jennifer, cautiously at first. I think it was rather novel for her to talk woman-to-woman to a male face. It was also novel for me to relax and talk about myself.

Once I moved into the school house and away from home I started searching for a support group and a source of estrogen to start the physical changes I wanted. Up to this time I had made no changes to my body except for shaving my legs and armpits. These were two things I felt I could do to 'feminize' my body that would not be visible to the casual observer.

Next was my clothing. During September and October my attire became more and more feminine to the point that people were turning to look. I was wearing high-waisted women's jeans with lime green or pink shirts. Combined with my long hair and white high-top women's sneakers I can see why they looked.

I was also taking my first tentative steps into the world fully dressed as a woman. I waited until dark, got dressed and put on make-up and a wig, and then walked for about a mile down the country road on which I lived, turned around and came home. Throughout these walks the adrenaline was coursing through me and I was ready to instantly jump off the road into the shadows if I heard a car.

When I first started going out in daylight I kept a low profile around my school house so that as few people as possible would notice when I made my ultimate change-over. I had to be careful because I was still working as a man but was now going to the support group and seeing Betty as a woman. It took some doing and was very trying on my nerves.

I put on my dress or skirt and a coat and then waited until no one was in sight and walked quickly to my car. Through the window, from the shoulders up, I still appeared to be male. After getting far enough from home so that I felt I would not be recognized I pulled over on the country road and put on my wig and make-up, then continued on my way.

I kept a diary and often referred to myself in it in the third person. As I grew and became more sure of my persona and how I wanted to be seen my name evolved from Jennie to Jenny, and finally Jen.

A week after I moved into the school house it was my birthday and I was excited at the prospect of at last celebrating it as a woman. I planned to go shopping and buy myself lots of presents for the house such as a microwave, a coffee maker, bed sheets and all the odds and ends that would make it mine. I recognized that there would be many hard times ahead but as much as I could I was going to stay optimistic.

Optimism was essential for me to succeed and was soon tested. My sister, Sally, died and I questioned my own mortality. I wondered when I would die, if someone would hit my car and end my life. I didn't want to die before I had a chance to live as a woman in public. I wanted to go shopping, visiting, see plays and movies, go swimming and so many other things. I resolved I must not die before I achieved those things that I had waited forty years for.

My biggest hurdle was how to remain patient and wait for the things I wanted, like a wig. I didn't know when I would get time to go and buy one but I wanted to squeeze it in before too long so that my short hair did not make me feel so masculine.

I had no idea when I would start on hormones but it could not be soon enough, the waiting was driving me crazy. I had been told that I had to go through tests. I had not realized that Betty wasn't licensed to prescribe drugs.

Seeing Betty at this time helped me to achieve the things I wanted in due course by taking one small step forward at each weekly visit. It was very hard. I wanted to get all the names I needed, make the appointments, and have surgery. I hated giving in to bureaucratic rules but it had to be done.

I was also worried about leaving Sam. I had to make sure that I spent time with him whenever I could and to let him know I still loved him. I had not yet told him that I was going to have a sex change. I decided to do it gradually, letting him witness my physical change in appearance and providing him with honest explanations.

My talks with Laurie continued and I found that she was scared of being left alone. She felt cheated that the man she had lived with had left her, and she would be a single mother with an uncertain future and income.

She also told me that nobody she had talked to thought that Sam should see me as a woman. Everyone she trusted, from school teachers to friends, had told her that he could not handle it, that it would devastate him. Also, Debbie, our next door neighbor, was the only person that she had talked to who thought that I could successfully live as a woman.

After hearing this I began to have serious doubts about the quality of my future life. I decided that very few people would ever understand what I was doing. I still had low self-esteem and I came to the conclusion that no one would ever live with a forty-year-old transgendered woman, let alone have sex with her. I pictured myself living alone and growing old by myself, separated from my family and everyone I loved.

Depression was creeping in and I had to take special care to ward it off. I sat down and went through all the positive aspects of my life. I recounted all I had achieved in life, specifically what I had achieved towards gender reassignment surgery. I considered living alone and not having sex again. I listed many people who lived alone and did not see the lack of sex as a problem. I had never enjoyed it anyway.

Twelve days after I moved into the school house I drove down to Boston and spent the night with my sister-in-law, Barb. She was very supportive and it was good to be with her and her family. I am sure that she had reservations about what I was doing but she at least appeared to see my side. She was a girl-friend, and I needed one.

The next morning, Saturday, I drove into town and bought a wig. I was not sure how much I liked it but the options were limited. I called a couple of places who curtly told me that they only did 'therapeutic wigs for women.' The shop I finally found was down a dark passage on the second floor of an old building in Boston. The door was unmarked except for the name of company and I had to ring until someone came and unlocked it.

There were rows and rows of flamboyant wigs in every style lined up on Styrofoam heads along the walls, with large mirrors with chairs in front of them. An older woman ran the shop. After she let the only other customer out, she locked the door behind her and asked what style I wanted. Since I was dressed as a man I explained I was transgendered and wanted something fairly plain that would not make me conspicuous.

I settled on a shoulder length auburn wig, close to my own coloring and offered a credit card to pay for it. She refused, saying she only accepted cash. I came up twelve dollars short, but the panic and sorrow in my face must have showed because she let me take the wig with a promise that I would mail the balance.

I left with my wig, still unsure how suitable it looked. I didn't want to go out in public and make a fool of myself. I didn't mind if I was seen as an unfortunately ugly woman, but I didn't want to be seen as 'a man wearing a dress.'

On the return drive from Boston I put on a skirt and my new wig and drove all the way to the highway overlook, about ten miles from home, before I thought I should change. It was a wonderful drive and I felt comfortable and relaxed.

Looking back at photos taken at that time I can see why my family and friends were concerned. I was wearing women's clothes and affecting the mannerisms and voice of a woman but I had not started taking hormones. My facial features had not yet started to soften. For people who did not know me the effect, now that I had a wig, was acceptable but for those who did know me the look was very much 'John in drag.'

As if to prove to myself that I was passable I sat on my front verandah with my wig on and wearing a corduroy skirt and a pink turtleneck. A teacher from the Mountain School came to the door and asked for permission to walk across the fields beside the house and did not seem put out at seeing me. Maybe he was being polite or just did not care but I felt as though he had not noticed anything untoward. It was a good experience, there was no adrenaline rush and, in general, I felt very comfortable.

I still had not been seen in my neighborhood as a woman. I wondered if I now had the courage to go down and get my mail from the post office as Jennifer. I knew I would have to force myself to try such things. Then I had another thought. Now that people were seeing me as a woman, how much longer would it be before I could no longer be seen in public as a man? Could John and Jennifer live in town as two separate people? And if so, for how long? Not long, I felt.

As I sat on the deck of the school house watching cars go by, I wondered what the people saw. A man or a woman?

I was thinking too much, analyzing too much. I wanted to make the final change and never go out in public as John again. But I had to wait. I was still working as a man and committed to the job until the end of October.

Thoughts kept racing through my head. I wanted to know where my need for my own life began and my concern for others ended? Was it time for me to announce my intentions to the world, make the change without waiting for work to end? I felt that maybe I was just tantalizing my family with the thought that I may not start living openly as a woman after all. Would it be kinder to end their waiting and doubting immediately with an irrevocable move? The truth of the matter was that I was just impatient. I could barely wait a minute longer.

Yet the prospect was still scary. Some days I wanted to stop because the task seemed so daunting. I would have to start my whole life over as a new person and develop a new network of contacts and supports that we all take for granted. But all the time I was growing and changing. I already had the first person in my new network in Betty, my counselor. A new life with new challenges was ahead of me. I had gone too far now to turn back. I had to go on strongly believing in myself.

I was very dependent on Betty during this transition. For the period between July 1990 and January 1991, I was seeing her at least twice a week. As I progressed this decreased to once a week, with the occasional emergency visit, until November 1991 when I was down to seeing her once every two weeks. This continued throughout 1992 until, from mid-December, I only saw her when I felt I had a special need, perhaps once a month, or less.

When I reached the point of looking for a support group and access to the physical changes, it again took many phone calls and chasing false leads. Betty and I both called the local area until she finally located a source that eventually led me to the people I needed.

I was moving forward again. I called the New Haven, Connecticut, contact Betty had found and she passed me on to a doctor in Hartford who passed me on to another person and finally I found the XX Club, a transgender support group, and made plans to go to their next meeting which fortunately was the following weekend. It had taken me three weeks to locate them. My need to progress was so great that if I had had to wait more than a few days to visit them I would have been a wreck.

I hoped that I had finally found the door behind which lay all my dreams. Over the years I had followed many false leads to get to that door. How many times had I backed away from others as I progressed? A career guidance course had told me that one of my qualities was perseverance. I knew I possessed it in spades. Without it I would have given up my quest years ago.

The night before I went to my first meeting of the XX Club the radio played "House of The Rising Sun." It was one of my favorites along with "St. James Infirmary Blues." It was an auspicious sign for the next day.

The support group was in Hartford. It was the nearest group to Vermont and one of only three anywhere near me. The other two were in Boston and New York City. If the weather was good and I could exceed the speed limit, it was still a three hour drive on the interstate. As it turned out I did not go very often.

On the first visit the day was wet and cold and after getting dressed up in a comfortable skirt and pink wool sweater over a turtleneck top, I headed down the interstate only to run into a police road block looking for illegal immigrants coming across the border from Canada. Not only did I not look like John, as it said on my driver's license, I did not even have 'his' green card with me. I was in a long queue of cars. I couldn't go back or turn around so I just moved slowly along until I reached the police officer. He smiled and asked me where I lived and where I was going, and then said, "Have a nice day," and waved me through.

The further I went the heavier the rain got and it made the traveling difficult, especially as the roof of the Alfa was leaking and in wet weather the car was prone to stopping unexpectedly as water somehow got into the electrical system.

When I got to Hartford I cruised around until I found a spot on the street to park and walked to the hall where the meeting was being held. They were an interesting group. If I had met any of them on the street, I would have questioned the gender of only one. Everyone else passed as fairly unremarkable women. There were even two very masculine looking female-to-male members of the Club.

After an hour or so of people offering suggestions and talking about their progress, Canon Jones, one of the facilitators, and I left for an interview. I had told my story to so many people that by then it was becoming somewhat intrusive. I wanted them to see what I wanted to do and let me get on with it. I understood that they wanted to make sure I was sincere and knew the ramifications of what I planned to do, but I was getting sick of it all.

Membership in the group was restricted to transgendered

people and at each meeting there were different people. Members were mainly male-to-female but there were always one or two who were female-to-male. We were all at varying degrees of change, some people being post-operative while others were obviously on the very start of their transition and extremely nervous. They would sit, as I had done at my first meeting, fidgeting with their hands and not knowing where to look. Those who had been attending for some time talked to them and tried to make them feel welcome, but the tension remained obvious from their tight lips and darting, evasive eyes.

Young people told how they had been kicked out of the house and had no job or place to live. Older people came with stories of a lifetime of dreaming that ended in the compromise of living alone, working as a man by day and living as a woman by night, in the privacy of their house or apartment. Young business women came and went, divine in the success of transition. They encouraged everyone with stories of life in the television industry or senior management. Middle-aged women told stories of changing on the job, retaining contacts with customers and employers, while reconstructing their lives around an old framework.

It was interesting to see the people who were changing female to male. While I was trying to grow breasts they were attempting to hide theirs by disguising the bulges with cigarette packets or pens stuffed into their shirt pockets.

The commitment of people like Canon Jones to help us in those early days of transition was remarkable. There were very few kudos in the job, and yet he gave his time and energy for many years, gently supporting those who needed it, and trying to direct and contain others. Some of the people at the meetings were angry and recounted how they had threatened to 'punch-out' those who ridiculed them in public or at work. Others were scared. They had received threatening phone calls late at night and menacing letters stuffed anonymously into their letter boxes. Some were devastated. One told how she had lost custody of her child after the death of a supportive ex-wife with whom she had been living. The in-laws were now in court attempting to withdraw her visitation rights. Somehow Canon Jones and those around him at the XX Club guided us all.

The time was coming for me to make my final change and I chose October 26, the day my seasonal job ended, as the last day that I would ever go out in public as John. I would have been wiser to wait until I was on hormones for a while but I was sick of waiting. I had been waiting for forty years and I wasn't going to wait a day longer than was absolutely necessary. I was fired up and nothing was going to stop me. I did, however, recognize that I would still need to adhere to the guidelines followed by those in Hartford, if I wanted to get surgery.

Before a reputable surgeon would perform my sex-change operation I had to comply with what is known as the Harry Benjamin Guidelines. Harry Benjamin was the first doctor to study transgendered people when, in 1949, one of the participants in the Kinsey Sexuality Studies insisted that, despite the fact that she was physically male, she was in fact female. This person was referred to Dr. Benjamin and, over a period of years working with similar people, he formulated the basic guidelines of treatment that were necessary to ensure that a person was fully aware of what it meant to have sex reassignment surgery.

The team in Hartford followed these guidelines. I had to be seen by Canon Jones, a psychologist, a psychiatrist, and an endocrinologist. If the group considered me truly transgendered, then they would agree to prescribe hormones and then monitor me for a period of twelve months. During that time I had to participate in the community and earn an income. It was not enough to just sit at home waiting or to live part-time in my old role. I had to prove to them that I could live and function in the community as a woman.

At the end of the twelve month supervision, if I still wanted it, they would give me a letter of recommendation to a doctor saying that I had been under their care and that they believed I should be accepted for surgery.

During this period I was very careful not to tell any of the

103

team that I was a lesbian. I had been warned that it was the aim of most assessment teams to turn out what they considered 'perfect women.' I never asked the Hartford team's view, but to most teams at that time, a 'perfect' woman was one who wanted to settle down with a man. I believed that if I told the team that I wanted to sleep with a woman after surgery, they would have believed that I was not truly transgendered, and would not have authorized the surgery. This view is slowly changing but, even now, being a lesbian only adds more difficulties to what is already a long and emotionally intrusive process.

By the end of September I had made all the necessary arrangements to get tested by the medical team in Hartford. My first visit was to be on October 10 for blood tests and psychological interviews. If all went well, I could go before the panel at their meeting in early November.

At the time I was too worried about the outcome of all the meetings to write about them in my diary. I did not want to jinx them in any way by talking about them.

As I waited for October 10 and my visit to Hartford I began making more forays into the community as Jennifer. Usually these were done in conjunction with visits to Betty, after which I headed for the shopping mall. On one such expedition I shopped first for some panty hose and got a pleasant "have a nice day" from the clerk. Next I found a watch and was told "thank you, ma'am," which made me feel absolutely wonderful. Finally I bought a purse and was asked if I wanted to take out a charge account.

I was finding very quickly that it was best if I presented myself confidently and believed in myself. I ended up using the phrase "I have the right" as an aid to remind me that most of my insecure feelings were unwarranted. As long as I was confident, and considerate of other people's temporary uncertainty and doubt when they met me, I would receive the benefit of the doubt.

I used store windows as a mirror to watch how people reacted to me. Did anyone stare as they passed? They did, but very rarely.

I had to contain my urge to discard John immediately and enjoy my new freedom from that day on. Now that my closet door was wide open I had to remain in control and finish my commitments before I rushed through it. I decided, however, that I did not need to wait for the team in Hartford to legitimize me at the November meeting. I resolved to stick to my plan of changing at the end of October.

October 10 finally arrived and I was seen by the members of the counseling group in Hartford. I received their informal verbal approval to go on hormones, but I had to wait a month for their formal go-ahead and the prescription for the needed hormones.

I was ecstatic at being approved and settled down to wait one more month. Later that night I woke at 4 a.m. petrified that I would either not get the hormones, or worse still, that I would die before I got a chance to live as I wanted. I was scared of dying, and yet I believed myself capable of suicide if I had to spend the rest of my life as a man. I eventually calmed down and resolved that I had to remain optimistic. But at times, with no one to convince me otherwise, it was hard.

I kept pushing on and the next day I went shopping. I made one bad mistake on this trip which I learned not to repeat. That morning I had only used the electric razor and I felt very uncomfortable with the amount of shadow it left. I was feeling tremendous stress living as a woman in some areas of my life and a man in others. When passing between one area and another in 'inappropriate' attire I was always looking out for familiar faces and cars that should be avoided. It was all very tiresome but the end of October would bring the dual lifestyle to an end.

My mood swings at this time were extreme. By 8 p.m. on the same day of my 4 a.m. panic attack, I was rock and rolling to the radio with happiness. If anyone had come to the door I would probably have been locked up. I was singing out of tune, and dancing up on the balls of my feet and swinging around the room.

On October 20 my landlady and her husband, who lived in

Boston, came by. I decided I had to tell her about my change. I told her I was going to be living as a woman and next time she saw me I would be Jennifer. She was very supportive, though obviously somewhat shocked. I felt I had to tell her out of courtesy and to warn her in case some of her local friends spoke to her about me. We had a good chat and as she and her husband drove off I was sure they would be discussing it.

Chapter Nine

On October 26, 1990, I became Jennifer for good.

I made the change quickly and completely. I gave the black Alfa Romeo convertible that was so well known in the neighborhood to Laurie and bought a Subaru four-wheel-drive station wagon. All signs of John were now gone and I had to steel myself never to go out again as a man. It was then that I really had to be brave. I started going into stores, meeting old friends, making new ones, developing new skills as Jennifer and discarding old habits. I had stepped straight into the deep end. Most of the family said I was crazy. They could still only see me as John in a dress. Betty was supportive and said I could do it.

Over the next few weeks I made lots of short forays into the world, and since I was accepted, my trips became longer and more frequent. Shopping in the anonymity of the mall was one thing, but now I had to go to the local general store where I was well known as John. Those first weeks, it was hard, and many months later it was still not easy, but I did it.

I went through my closets and gave away the last of my men's clothes. At last I had turned the corner and it was men's clothes going into the charity collection bin, not women's.

From then on I had to go everywhere as a woman. "Had to" because I still had a certain amount of fear of going out. I often had to force myself to go into a shop. I knew that my fear would subside eventually, but since I had never enjoyed crowds, I knew it would take some time.

Laurie had, with my permission, started telling our mutual

friends about my change. A growing number of people expected to see 'the new girl on the block.'

I started to look for a new job. As Laurie pointed out at the time, this would not be easy. I was now a woman and the area I was living in was economically depressed with very few jobs. I had confidence, however, and even if it was initially only a volunteer position I found I was sure that it would lead to something satisfying.

I still had not told Sam exactly what I was planning and he had not seen me as Jennifer. Sam and I had spoken about my wanting to live as a woman before I moved out of the family home and I was honest with him and answered all his questions as clearly as I could, considering he was only nine. I told him what I was going to do and how much it meant to me. It was very hard to tell him and I did it as gently as I could. We both cried and as we talked it became apparent that his main concern was that I would go away and he would never see me again. When I assured him that I was not going away, and that we would still see lots of each other, he brightened up.

On November 3, he and Laurie came over for a 'formal introduction.' A major hurdle had been surmounted.

During those first months of transition I actively searched out activities that would force me out of the house and back into a productive life. I had to start earning some money as I was living on my savings. I knew that the only way that I would succeed was if I really pushed myself hard and took all the risks necessary to become accustomed to my new lifestyle. I felt that there was little chance of finding full-time work immediately and, anyway, I wanted the flexibility to be able to continue my counseling and writing. I looked for volunteer work where I could set my own hours.

I had heard of a state-run agency called Step-Up for Women that trained women for plumbing, house building, electrical wiring and other non-traditional jobs. Without telling them I was transgendered, I wrote and volunteered my services, explaining that I had experience in both the building industry and in working with people. It took a long time for them to reply, but they finally did and I started working in the office doing filing and mailings and putting up advertising posters. After a month I felt I should tell them about my background. They were wonderfully supportive and my working relationship with them went on unchanged.

My family in America, however, had only known me as my birth-allocated gender, and even when I became reasonably passable in public all they could see was that person they used to know. They were so sure that everyone else could also see through my new image that they did not want to be seen in public with me. I was no longer invited to go out with them. If they were expecting visitors I got some unsubtle hints that they would prefer it if I left. I don't want to suggest that their reactions were unreasonable in those early days, but it repeatedly damaged my fragile self-confidence and, with it, my self-esteem.

To get through this period I took to writing more notes to myself. "You have the right, you are a woman," I wrote. And, "You must succeed at any cost." I pasted these notes up where I needed them, on the mirror and the door of my clothes closet. I also put up warning notes over the phone that said, "The name is Jenny!" The one by the front door just read, "Make up?" There were so many new things to remember.

I finally reached November 15, the day when I would get formal approval for the all important prescription that would start changing the physical appearance of my body. Unlike the time all those years ago in Australia when I was not ready to begin, this time I could hardly wait.

I received 'the pill' and a formal letter signed by the head of the team monitoring my change. The letter explained that should my right to be in public as a woman ever be questioned, I was transgendered and was being monitored by the Hartford medical group in preparation for 'gender reassignment surgery' and hence the reason for my wearing women's clothing while still ostensibly a man.

Unfortunately, this trip was followed by a number of very

down times, including a family Thanksgiving to which I was not invited, and Fred's birthday lunch to which Jenny was not welcome but John was. The hardest thing was I had to get up each morning and keep fighting. I longed for an easy few months. I didn't want to keep struggling. I wanted to be a woman and not worry about passing. I was so sick of fighting to be accepted. But I kept going and set some very strict rules for myself. The main one was that I was not going to weaken and dress as a man on those occasions when I was not welcomed as Jenny. In those first few months this was an option I refused to take on the grounds that it would be a retrograde step that would show others that I was not entirely serious in my resolve to change. Most importantly to me, I knew I was a woman, and so I was not going to dress as a man just to make those around me feel more comfortable.

Chapter Ten

Unless it's a costume party, anyone who goes out in public wearing the clothes normally associated with the opposite gender worries about 'passing.' Passing is the ability to be out in public without those around you believing you are inappropriately dressed for your birth-assigned gender. For a transgendered person this need to pass is particularly important because we are planning to live that way for the rest of our lives. For some, like myself, it is comparatively easy to pass. Others, due to physical size or facial shape, may never pass easily, even after major cosmetic surgery. These people are no less female than I am, yet they will always have to struggle against insensitive people who mock their appearance.

For the first months after my changeover most of my time and energy was taken up with learning how to pass in public as a woman. I rarely went visiting socially and lived pretty much as a hermit. I still went bird watching in the woods, but I did it alone.

After starting on hormones I began a chart to graph the physical changes that were occurring in my body. Each week I measured my hips, waist and breasts with a dressmaker's tape and marked down the gradual change in my outline. Over the ensuing months I joined each successive dot on the graph and realized with pleasure how steadily the hormones were changing the shape of my body.

I started to go out socially in public. One of the first times was to have lunch at a restaurant with Priscilla, a friend of

Betty's. It was the longest that I had sat in view of a group of people. It was a great learning experience, and although some people did look over and stare a little, they soon went back to their meals and conversations. My appearance was obviously acceptable and I had an enjoyable lunch.

After being excluded from Thanksgiving and then seeing a letter that my father had written to Laurie in which he told her that he could only see me as a man in a dress wearing too much make-up, I hit bottom and experienced a deep bout of depression.

It started in the afternoon, after reading my father's letter, and spiraled down. I walked around and around the small living room of my house and screamed and threw myself on the couch. I wanted to know where my life was going. I felt totally alone and desperate. I was forty-four years old and unemployed. My savings was dwindling and now my father was sending hateful letters.

In the evening I started drinking vermouth and writing a letter to Betty. I told her how I felt like a child who was too scared to go out the front gate. Inside the gate there was no danger, no responsibility. "Mummy will look after me, I can hide behind her" was the way I felt. I wanted the security of childhood and freedom from struggle. I was sick of fighting. Every day I got up and put on a front of confidence for all those people who said I could not succeed, including sometimes, even myself. I wanted it all to end. I wanted my life to be normal and calm. I wanted friends and laughter.

I continued drinking and writing as a means of venting my frustration and despair. What I really wanted was to lose physical control and throw the vermouth bottle through the front window of the house, but I couldn't, my upbringing wouldn't let me. I felt I would get into trouble and only have to clean up the mess in the morning. So I screamed and stamped around the house, then wrote out the depression, instead of venting it in violence.

I ranted onto the paper, questioning the meaning of unconditional love and exploring the idea of suicide. I considered leaving my family and running away to live alone and unknown; starting a new life in seclusion in a corner of the world where no one would ever find me. I wrote vaguely about self worth and future prospects and spewed out a list of sentiments on how I felt about my father and sisters. In the end the letter ran to some four pages and was an incoherently garbled mixture of self pity, anger, frustration and alcohol.

By 8 p.m. the bottle of vermouth was empty and I was drunk, so I went to bed and slept off the remains of my depression. The next morning I posted the letter and got on with my life.

Purging my feelings by writing the letter allowed me to reexamine my thoughts and emotions in the sobriety of the next day. My opinions had not changed since the night before, but they had moderated. Within a few days my memory of the night had faded and I was back on track and concentrating on the task of living and assimilating into society.

At my next meeting with Betty, however, I discovered that the letter had worried her more than I expected. The session included close questioning about its content and a suggestion that I consider joining a local AA group. I must have convinced her that my extreme depression was a passing event but, as always, I realized some hours later that my drinking was still something I needed to monitor closely. From then on I made it a rule never to have more than one bottle of wine or vermouth, or six cans of low alcohol beer in the house at any time, and never hard liquor. I had never liked whisky, especially since I had become very sick more than once on overproof dark rum as a teenager, so I could no longer even drink it.

I still found it very hard to go out in public and took a lot of time getting dressed. If I so much as forgot to put on earrings or lipstick I panicked and felt I looked too masculine; if I was within five minutes of home I turned around and went back and put them on. I had to be one hundred percent comfortable with my appearance in order to go out.

After a month on hormones my diary showed that there were some definite changes taking place in my body. My skin had dried out somewhat and my breasts had started to grow. I was also more emotional. As the changes progressed I became more willing to go out and enjoy the world. I was invited to some local Christmas events and I resolved to go to them.

I recalled my first tentative steps up the road in the dark, which, both figuratively and literally, gave me moral strength, and reminded me how much easier it was now, even though it had only been forty-six days since I had stopped living as a man.

To help encourage my self-confidence I marked the calendar in days since I had left my family house on Gove Hill, days since I had first appeared as Jenny, and days since I had started the pill. None of them had hit three figures.

Once I started my change-over I rarely saw any of the mutual friends Laurie and I had once had. I did not know how I would be accepted by them and was scared of being rejected. I also felt that as Laurie was still seeing them it would be easier for her if I were not present. On a couple of occasions Laurie specifically arranged, without my knowledge, to have me included in some party or gathering. Her support for me was always wonderful and my transition would have been a lot harder without her help. It was Laurie who encouraged me to go to a concert with her and her boyfriend, Rick. I met a lot of old friends that night for the first time as Jennifer. I was so shy I spoke to very few. Mostly I just waved or smiled.

The concert turned out to be a mixed success. The music was great but I had never had so many people stare at me. I realized that I needed, in those early days of my transition, to consider the lighting before I went anywhere. The concert was at a mall and the lighting, which produced lots of shadows, showed up all my worst features.

Soon after starting on hormones I learned the cathartic effect tears can have. Quite often I became so depressed that I collapsed on the couch and sobbed uncontrollably for no apparent reason. I had always been taught not to show any emotions, even when alone. When the tears finally ended I felt that all my emotions had been washed out, and I became very calm and relaxed. It was a deep inner feeling, as though everything had become very clean and clear and coated with a light dusting of euphoria.

I also allowed myself the pleasure of reading or day dreaming without feeling guilty that I was wasting time. After one night of freezing rain, which covered the roads in black-ice and made it too dangerous to drive, I spent the whole day reading and writing in my diary. I felt that I was wasting time, that I should have been out in public and looking for work, but I enjoyed the day.

I started to make some friends in the local lesbian community and found that a lot of their struggles with family acceptance and rejection were similar to mine. Two of these people were involved in the Metropolitan Community Church (M.C.C.), a church for gays and lesbians, and I decided to attend their service on Christmas Eve. I hoped that they would be a potential support in lieu of a local XX branch. At M.C.C. I was introduced first hand to the AIDS crisis. One of the people there had just lost a partner to the disease and it was very moving hearing him talk about it. Until then I knew very little about AIDS or how it was affecting the gay community.

There were very few self-help books specifically for transgendered people, but I found that books written for the gay community about coming out were in many ways applicable to me. They gave me insight into what it was going to be like for me now that I was starting to live a lesbian lifestyle in the general community.

Looking back it is interesting to realize that I never considered keeping my lesbian lifestyle in the closet. For some reason it never entered my head that I should hide my sexuality, possibly because I was so sick of hiding my gender dysphoria.

Christmas was approaching and on December 21 I went over to our house at Gove Hill to help Rick, Sam, and Laurie decorate the tree. It was pleasant and the first time that year that I had felt any Christmas spirit. Rick was living at Gove Hill for the Christmas holidays and during that time I visited regularly and we all went sledding, had snowball fights, and sat together around the fire.

It had been a long time since I had seen Laurie so relaxed. Rick was sleeping with her in our old bed and he and Sam were getting on wonderfully. I still had some slim hope that Laurie and I would get back together but as I sat watching them I saw that this was highly unlikely. We had once planned to grow old together and live in a cottage in the woods surrounded by wild and domestic animals. Everything had changed and I was becoming less sure as the days went on that I even wanted to move back to Gove Hill.

I was adamant that I should not 'waste' time during my transition, and sometimes I found that first winter to be a frustrating time. I didn't have a job and there were only three other reasons to go out. The first was to go walking or cross- country skiing. Because of the cold, and because everyone else had a job, I had to do it alone. It was usually a brief excursion.

The second reason was job hunting. It was a draining exercise that was best done in conjunction with the third— shopping. This was by far the most enjoyable, but it cost money and, being unemployed, money was a commodity in short supply.

I found it easier to stay home and develop "cabin fever." I could hardly wait until the spring when I was sure I would find a job and be able to take long evening walks through the woods chasing spring warblers.

In the beginning I never knew how to introduce myself on

the phone. Once, when I called Cassie, Laurie's sister, I didn't know whether to say Jenny or John. With Laurie or Sam I just said, "Hi, it's me." Outside the family it depended if the person had met me as Jenny or not. On all my Christmas cards to Australia for 1990 I signed, Love John. Fred and Marje called me John, to which I responded. Betty had said I would probably have to give some sort of deadline after which I would not answer to John, and I decided that that time would be somewhere early in the New Year. I did it gradually and respected people's attempts at remembering to use my new name.

Now that I was obviously not male, it was not only inappropriate but potentially dangerous for someone to call me John in public. I had heard stories in Hartford of people being bashed for being transgendered, although it had not happened to me. I was conscious of how I looked, so if someone stared or laughed, as sometimes happened, I lost my nerve and headed back to the security of home. After such an occurrence it took me some time to rebuild my confidence to the level it was before the event.

Of everyone, Sam was the most careful to use my new name. When someone in the family used the wrong name or pronoun, he rounded on them and said seriously, "Her name is Jenny!"

One of my strongest defenses was a smile. It was absolutely vital. I found it hid insecurity and made me feel better able to face the world. People also like to relate to a happy face. They will do more for you and be more supportive than when you are frowning.

The atmosphere that first Christmas was good and I did not feel as uncomfortable as I thought I might. Sam was a great joy and apart from his natural fear of being seen by one of his friends while he was with me, he was very supportive. Willie, his six-year-old cousin, was there and did not bat an eyelash and called me Jenny from the moment I walked in. Tom, Willie's older brother, who was eight, was not as sure but ended up sleeping over one night at Gove Hill with Sam and me.

By New Year's Eve day the strain of socializing was beginning to show and I sulked all morning. Laurie and Rick invited

117

me out to lunch but I said no and sulked. Then I changed my mind, determined to overcome my mood. There was snow on the road and the sales were on in the shops. People were walking around wrapped up in winter coats and the sky was clear and blue. We sat together at a restaurant and had lunch, then cruised some shops. I found a pair of fur-lined boots, a new dress, and a top, all on sale. It showed me again how important it was to retain a positive attitude.

As well as making sure that I had good assistance during my transition I did my best to support Sam in every way possible. I not only sought professional advice for him, but always asked him how he was feeling and what he wanted. He was now nine and I felt he was capable of understanding and having input into matters where he was directly concerned. I was also adamant that he would always be told the truth about what was happening. At no time did I want him to feel that he had been deceived.

The main concern Laurie and I had was how Sam's friends at school would treat him if and when they found out about me. So far there had been no problem, but only a handful of them knew. Only time would tell if he would be persecuted. This was my biggest fear about making my change without leaving the area. We had checked with a child psychologist and we were assured that it was best for Sam that I stayed, but there were times when I wondered. All we could do was seek professional advice and go with it.

I told Sam that he was totally free to tell me if he felt uncomfortable while we were out together. He did so more than once and I changed my plans to suit him. In this matter he was the boss and I respected his wishes completely. I also allowed him to remove and play with my wig when we were at home so that he could see that I was the same person underneath.

I also kept a safe distance from any situation that could have made things hard for him. I did not go near his school or his local store, nor did I go to town or social meetings. It was a small price to pay for his security and comfort.

Throughout the period of my change-over I found the best advice I could. My actions were not isolated and I had to think of others with every move I made. My family had to be treated tenderly. Strangers had to see that I was not a threat. I had to remember that what I was doing was totally alien to most people and that I was likely to be the first transgendered person they had ever knowingly met.

Early in January 1991 Sam told me that I was looking more like a woman to him. This gave me quite a boost. Rather than worrying how I looked I needed to get on with the job of living. I knew there were plenty of people with more difficult appearance problems than I had and they lived with it. This was easy to say but very hard to do.

As each day passed it became more natural for me to move about in public as a woman. Some shop attendants were getting to know Jenny and it was nice to just feel accepted. The less self-conscious I became the more convincing I became, and the less confusing I was to other people. I was also worrying less about what other shoppers thought about me.

Sometimes after seeing Betty, I didn't feel as though I had gained anything from my visit, and then I'd remember a small thought or word from her office and something would click into place. A whole flood of information would flow clearly to me. Even my dreams were different. I woke up one morning and knew that a change had occurred. John had been replaced by Jennifer in my dreams.

I kept up an active pace and found that my assimilation went faster and easier when I did. For every day I hid myself in the house I lost about two days of confidence.

By mid-January it was time to start making the legal changes that would be necessary for my transition. My friends gave me the name of a lawyer in the lesbian community and I called her and told her on the phone that I was transgendered and needed help with the legal aspect of my change-over. When we met later she was surprised. She had been expecting a female-to-male-transgendered. My voice on the phone had sounded like a woman, she said. I was happy.

Being so involved with how my change-over was affecting me and my immediate family, I lost sight of how it was affecting my friendships. I had cut myself off from old friends, leaving it up to them to contact me if they wanted to renew our friendship. It would have been better if I had contacted the closer ones and asked what sort of information, if any, they wanted from me. But my self-confidence was still extremely fragile and the fear of calling someone and asking if they were still a friend was too great. It would have cost me a lot if they had rejected me. In the end some friends did back away but the vast majority remained supportive.

A friend, Chris, called in late January and voiced the concerns of others. He was having some friends over for dinner and was feeling unsure about inviting me. He didn't know if I would be comfortable; he was concerned that he would say something wrong and embarrass both himself and me. I reassured him that I was perfectly relaxed with my change and that I would love to come for dinner. I also told him that I would not be offended if someone used my old name. I knew how hard it was to change.

In early February I had my first holiday as Jennifer. I spent a weekend in Provincetown and stayed in an apartment owned by a friend. It was right on the waterfront and had a huge view over the bay. At high tide the water lapped at its foundations. In the evenings I sat and read and watched the seals rolling and playing in the calm water inside the breakwater. During the day I wandered around, ate at the small cafes and generally had a quiet weekend exploring and enjoying being alone and away by myself. I was still not comfortable wearing pants, I thought they made me look too masculine, so I wore a blue denim skirt and sneakers. In Provincetown, a town full of gay people, the skirt wasn't fooling anyone but me. It was an important delusion for me though. It was very important to feel passable, even if I was not.

For the whole weekend I barely spoke to anyone other than to order a meal or buy a gift. I was conscious that I was alone and try-ing a whole new experience. In the adjoining apartment there was a woman, also alone but with her dog, and whenever I saw her on her balcony I was tempted to wave or say hello, but never did. In the streets I walked along with my head down, looking as though I knew where I was going.

On the beach I walked for miles and loved it. Being February it was deserted and the small waves lapped the sand. A few sea ducks lay rafted off shore and occasionally one or two took off and flew low into the distance.

That night I had an early meal at a cafe and took some beer back to the apartment. I sat watching the lights of town and writ-ing poetry to the sound of classical music until well after mid-night.

Chapter Eleven

As I progressed through my transition many things changed in me, and in my outlook on life. I explored old feelings towards friends, family and myself, adjusting them continually as I came to terms with my transgenderism. When I started the transition I was very angry about the way I had been treated. As a result I used lower case letters when writing the names of family members who I believed had let me down, and for those occasions, especially 'christmas,' whose relevance to me had become tainted by society's hypocrisy.

I also decided that 'John' was someone from whom I wanted to divorce myself totally. I rejected everything that he had ever been or achieved. I denied his very existence, starting by degrading his name.

I was having trouble visiting my old home on Gove Hill too. When I entered the grounds I resumed a male role. I found it uncomfortable and became happier being away from there. Even so I had the underlying knowledge that if Laurie had asked me to move back to the house I probably would have tried it, undoubtedly ending up regretting it.

What I really wanted was for Laurie to find a husband. I wanted to have the last of my male duties taken from me. I didn't want to lose the security of her friendship, or the link to the past, but I wanted to relinquish my male role. I knew it would not be good for me to push her too hard, so I concentrated on being more feminine when I was at Gove Hill.

It was this discarding of my trained masculinity that proved difficult. When I was in an old John environment, Jennifer receded. It was even harder to keep my voice at a higher pitch, as though I was still trying to deny my new self while I was with my family.

I believe the reason for this denial was a deep desire to try and show the family that the old John was still there, just beneath the surface of the new me. Instead it reinforced their belief that I could not succeed in changing my role. As a result I made it harder for myself. I tried to stop slipping back when I went to Gove Hill. Jenny was here forever and the sooner that the change happened everywhere the better.

The long, cold months of New England winter, while beautiful, sometimes kept me inside where I had the time to explore my own life and future needs. I rarely wasted any of this time and spent many hours reading and learning, as well as writing in my diary.

There were some very good bookshops nearby and an excellent library so I spent many hours broadening my knowledge. I rarely read any novels and restricted myself to what I felt were educational books. A lot of these I bought from a bookstore in Hanover. Its basement had a wide selection of women's books as well as many by and about lesbian and gay people. The owners of the school house had also left some good books, including biographies and autobiographies.

By February I was facing the problem of who I should tell about my change, if anyone. I had made two close friends, Mig and Emmie, and I wondered if I should tell them. In the end, I didn't. Then there was my neighbor Nora. I did tell her. And how about the parents of Sam's friend Nathan? I knew that the parents of Sam's close friends needed to know, but the fear in coming out to them was degrading. I told Nathan's mother so that Nathan could come to my place and play, and Sam told Nathan. I knew that I was not a risk, no more than any other woman that their children might meet, and yet I felt compelled to come out to them and ask permission to be with their child. It was so intrusive, yet our society's homophobic fears made it essential. As Sam said one day, "It's all so complicated."

One of my first priorities after deciding to change over, but before actually doing it, was to start electrolysis treatment for the removal of facial hair. I was fortunate that my facial hair grew very slowly. If I shaved with a razor blade in the morning I had no trouble being in public all day. But I wanted to complete the electrolysis treatment as soon as possible.

Electrolysis is a slow process and on some people, treatment can leave nasty red blotching for a day or two, and each hair has to be treated more than once.

I found a very nice electrolysist who had worked with two other transgendered people. My first forty-five minutes were not painful, although the swelling did not completely go down for 48 hours. After the first one or two treatments I had no reaction other than some slight reddening of the skin for an hour or so afterwards. I booked two one-hour visits each week, trying to get as much as possible done before summer. After the first few minutes I found that I could relax into a meditative state where I felt nothing more than the occasional prick and a pulling sensation as the hair came out. If I tried to talk I could feel the needle.

The electrolysis proceeded steadily and I could see some results after only a few weeks, but it went more slowly than I had expected, even though she was pulling out some 300 hairs an hour. After my seventh hour, which meant 2000 hairs, she was still working on my chin. I wanted her to tackle my throat next. I was wearing turtlenecks which I couldn't wear in the spring. With hindsight, electrolysis was the one thing I should have started before I began my transition, but I did not have the courage. I had over 250 hours of treatment before I was satisfied with the result.

Arriving for treatment one afternoon I had my first taste of harassment. I stopped to buy some milk and as I pulled out of the parking lot a truck pulled out after me. It followed me for some blocks and I watched the large man in the front seat as he drove up close behind me. When I turned into the electrolysist's lot he pulled up beside me and said, "Hi. I think I know you. Would you like to come have a drink?"

I had never seen him before and said, "I've written down your number. If I ever see you or your truck anywhere near me again, I will call the police."

He said, "Well, fuck you," and pulled away with his tires smoking.

After he had gone I went inside and watched to see if he came back, but he didn't.

My hair was getting long enough to consider discarding my wig. I began experimenting with hair styles and getting to know how I wanted to look. Stupidly I had had my hair cut the previous August because it was getting too long. It was probably my last attempt to remain as John. Even then I was denying what I had openly said I was going to do.

I decided that the wig had to go by the end of April when the weather got consistently warm. As people saw my new hair style and commented, I felt it would be a second coming out, which I was not looking forward to. I planned to make the change as late as possible.

When I was young people had commented on how wonderful my hair looked. Now it was fine, graying and receding. How I envied some of the young transgendered people in Hartford who had thick heads of hair. I knew mine would improve but it would never get back to its old self.

During the early transition period I had to remember to appear as a woman twenty-four hours a day. I had to be prepared to greet people at any hour. I had visitors as late as midnight, and it was hard to look pretty at that hour at the best of times. I could not afford to get up in the morning and lounge around without shaving, unless I wanted to pretend I was not home when the doorbell rang. As I became more comfortable with my new life and started to look and feel more feminine it became easier.

As each day went by I slowly discarded all the mental paraphernalia I had surrounded myself with in order to pass as a man. All the defense mechanisms that I had cultivated over the last forty years were no longer needed and my new persona was slowly emerging. It was not an easy task because many of those devices were subtle and ingrained. It was even hard to list them as individual items. They were all the little reactions and mannerisms, like a strong handshake and hiding tears, that went with my day-to-day life.

My old protective armor was falling away and, ever so steadily, a new, confident person was emerging. I could express all my emotions, both feminine and masculine, without the fear of being exposed. I felt I was beginning to relate to people from my true perspective and, conversely, they were finally relating to the real me. My true self was exploring new areas of human contact and not feeling rebuffed. It was this evolving mental freedom that I found the most liberating part of my transition.

As I dismantled my old behavior I became more and more self-confident. The changes were often subtle and it was sometimes not until afterwards that I realized I had handled something differently than I would have in the past. As I merged into the general community I was allowing myself to be part of it.

For my comparatively easy transition into the community I owe a great deal to the New England ethic of 'Do as you please, so long as it does not hurt anyone.' While shopping and going to restaurants, I appeared feminine enough to rarely turn a head. From those people who knew of the change, such as the bank manager and the staff at the general store, I received nothing but kindness and support.

One morning I walked into the post office with my heart in my throat and said to the postmistress, "Hi, I'm Jenny and I will be collecting the mail from now on."

Her response was, "That's okay by me." From then on she treated me as a woman.

Most New Englanders are truly kind and compassionate people and I am glad that I lived there. I am sure I was the topic of discussion at many dinner tables but I could accept that.

The first few times I told people that I was not the man I had once appeared to be, it was hard to find the right words. I also found that for many people there was a difference between hearing my news and actually seeing me. When someone heard my explanation and said "That's nice" I knew they had filed the information with other facts they did not want to confront. But when they saw me they had to confront an indisputable fact and figure out how they were going to handle it, and me. It was sometimes harder for them than me, and I had to be prepared for a variety of reactions.

Some people, after hearing my explanation, started out tolerant and then kept a distance. Other people wanted to know everything and I encouraged them to ask questions. And still others, lawyers and bank staff and some casual friends, only needed to know that I was changing. I tried to be kind and gentle, but I did not need their approval. Close friends needed further information on which to rebuild their ideas of who I had become.

Some people didn't need to know anything about my change. I didn't lie to them, but if they didn't ask, I didn't tell. It was a dilemma deciding whether to tell someone. I made friends with one woman, as a woman, and some time later, because I did not know if I was passing or not, I told her that I was transgendered. She had not suspected. I had not needed to tell her. We remained friends but the relationship changed, even if only in my mind, and I became less relaxed.

Children were often the easiest to tell. They had not learned prejudice and were prepared to accept me for myself. If I was friendly they reacted to that, unconcerned with complicated adult reactions like homophobia, protocol and gender roles. It was their parents who believed the worst.

I expected that one day I could stop deciding who needed what information. That day would be when all my old friends knew about my change and all my new friends wouldn't need to know. I would be Jennifer and always had been.

Money was the only other thing that was still a major problem. I had reached a point where I was working with a support group and a psychologist and living full-time as my female self. My counseling, my new wardrobe and my hormones had cost over six thousand dollars in twelve months. I had started electrolysis and had sought legal assistance for a name change and other legal matters that would require another nine thousand dollars over the next twelve months. Cosmetic surgery, if I had it, was a major expense I was hoping to avoid. The biggest single outlay of money would be my reassignment surgery which was approximately seven thousand dollars. I had been told that before they were finished most people spent twenty-five to thirty thousand. I never counted up what I spent, but I felt that this was a conservative estimate. And I was living on my savings which was dwindling fast.

Chapter Twelve

By March 1991 I had been on hormones for four months. After seventy days my breasts were developed enough that I would have made a strange sight if I were trying to live as a man. With little more than a wig, some make-up, and a pair of breast pads which I had made from the shoulder pad of a dress, I was physically small enough to pass in my new persona.

The hormones slowed my beard growth to the point where I could go twenty-four hours before I had a shadow. My waist had become more obvious and my hips were getting larger as the layers of body fat redistributed themselves. All in all it was a very pleasing change.

Mentally I had been a woman all my life so there was no problem there, other than the temporary feeling that everyone else thought that I was a man in a dress. I knew this would be a problem so I had tried to lessen its impact by talking to myself when I had worked on the market farm in 1989. I always addressed myself as Jenny. I concentrated on perfecting new mannerisms and body movements. I studied other women and read magazines to learn more about current fashions.

I considered my change to have started in January 1989 with my research at the Dartmouth medical library. Considering all the preparatory work, the medication had just been a formality. The only real mental change I noticed was that my passionate, destructive need to be a whole person was gone. I was finally living my life as I had always wanted—free to express my emotions without fear that I would embarrass myself. I could skip, laugh, dance or cry as the mood took me. I could finally live openly with body and mind expressing their true unified gender. This was the change I had been waiting for. The mental change was the liberation of my female emotions.

For the first time ever I was learning to love my body. I looked in the mirror and saw what I had longed for all my life.

Choosing clothes each morning was now fun. I no longer just got up and put on whatever was on the top of the pile. I selected items that went together, and often changed my mind and selected something else.

I liked being treated as a woman in public. I liked being called "Ma'am." I tried on dresses before I bought them. It was 'a kinder, gentler world.' I knew all about feminism, reduced wages and glass ceilings, but right then I was enjoying being an old-fashioned woman. Before the novelty wore off I intended to milk it for all it was worth.

One thing that remained constant throughout the years was my need to achieve. I needed to keep moving forward and attempting to improve my position. I was not content with the status quo. In the work environment I always wanted to improve the quality of my job. In my private life I looked for a resolution of my problems, even if it took years.

This drive proved very helpful during my transition. It gave me the strength to make endless phone calls and set up countless meetings as I searched for the right professionals to help me.

I had jumped precipitously into my new life and I had not considered how many ancillary changes would be necessary. Not only did I have a new persona, I had to establish a whole new network. This included everything from advising the post office to changing my name on my driver's license and credit cards and contacting doctors, the dentist, lawyers, and insurance agents.

In the case of my insurance agent and my bank, I kept the old contact and just changed my name. With other more personal connections, like the dentist and the doctor, I established new ones. I did this for two reasons. I wanted to allow Laurie and Sam to visit the ones we had jointly used. I didn't want them to feel as though they had to explain, or justify, my change. I also wanted to work with people who were tolerant of what I had done. For example, I needed a local doctor who could prescribe hormones for me. A female doctor who worked with a lot of the local lesbians had been recommended. She had never treated a transgendered person before, but she was happy to work with me. As with most of the professional people I had to deal with, I had to teach her initially and then later we both learned together.

I was still finding that absolute truth was not possible for me, despite my desire to stop lying about who I was. I now had a group of people who accepted me as a woman and I found I had to modify my stories so that I omitted facts that would give me away.

Sometimes, for convenience, I had no choice but to lie, but I began to wonder if people were seeing through the charade. Worse still, I worried that they were offended or insulted. How would they react when they found out? This dilemma came home on one occasion when I joined a women's book discussion group without divulging my background. Since we were just talking about books I did not see the need. Over a period of a few months though it became apparent to me that some members of the group were unhappy that I was there. The meetings got smaller and finally the group fell apart. It probably was not all due to me but there was enough evidence that I began to wonder.

Should I have asked if they minded having someone who was transgendered in their group? I could not go everywhere begging for acceptance. I had to make a judgment call and go with it. Sometimes I was right, occasionally I was wrong.

As Betty said, some things can be known without the fact being spoken. A friend can know, and I can know they know, and with this understanding a friendship can continue. However, if the other person is uncomfortable, and does not speak out, I can only proceed as politely and in as friendly a manner as I would in any other social situation.

As part of the Harry Benjamin requirements I had to retain contact with the group of professionals in Hartford. Because I was so far from them they allowed me to use my own network to some extent but I still had to report to them at least once every three months. Since my local network was very good, I felt that this was an imposition, but I was willing to do it because they were my key to having surgery. On April 15 I had my first quarterly check-up with the endocrinologist in Hartford, who determined that I was progressing well.

In April I started my first paid job. I had been buying clothes at a local recycled clothing store. During a conversation with the owner, Pat, she had mentioned that she would be looking for part-time help soon. Was I interested? I left my name and number, thinking I would never hear from her, but she called and offered me the job.

I did not want her to find out about me from a customer, so I told Pat about my past. She was good but I was still scared that something would go wrong. I thought she would tell me that she had changed her mind, but she didn't.

The store specialized in high quality used women's clothing, things Pat had bought or that were on consignment. It was a small shop but well-known and people came from all over to shop there.

Pat had a talent for decorating. Everything was presented elegantly. Wonderful period dresses and hats, gloves and other trimmings hung on the walls. The atmosphere was helped by the fact that the building was a classic old New England country store. Walking into the shop was like walking back in time. It had once been a butchers shop and the changing room was the old cool room. The door was over six inches thick.

I didn't earn much money working there but I got the job as a woman and was working as one—a huge boost for my morale. I loved the work and the interaction with customers.

After I started, Pat said that she wanted to tell Danette, the other employee, about me. We were good friends but I felt the recurrent fear that I would be rejected and asked to leave. As it happened Danette did not mind.

As far as I know during the whole time I worked at Pat's shop there was only one complaint. The husband of a customer tried to discourage Pat from hiring me. "You know you are taking a risk having that person work for you," he said to her. "Aren't you scared that someone will throw tomatoes or eggs at your shop?"

Working at Pat's store had another benefit that I had not foreseen. I was confronted with lots of women in a woman's realm. I was learning conversation techniques, fashion, clothing types, and deportment. I could not afford to relax my guard for a moment and it was paying off. I found that I used my higher voice at home without thinking about it. Also, after years of being told how poor my taste in clothes could be, I found that my ability to coordinate women's clothes was very good.

People came into the store and liked the clothes I selected for them. Even with my limited wardrobe I got compliments on what I wore.

That Easter Laurie, her parents and Sam went to Boston. I was invited but I decided to stay in Vermont and have a quiet time by myself. I finished work at Pat's store and went to Gove Hill to feed Laurie's horse and get the dog, which I was looking after.

Laurie had left a note with some candy and shampoo as an Easter gift. I read the note, ate some candy, and collected items to take back to my house. When I picked up the dish of candy I saw a small sachet that I recognized. Many years before, when Laurie and I had been living in Connecticut, my parents came to visit and we went to New York for the weekend. My mother wanted to buy something from Tiffany's as a memento of the weekend. Like the omelet in Maxim's, I remember her going into Tiffany's and buying a silver and crystal pendant, something that she could afford, just because she wanted something from there.

After her death, Laurie chose the pendant during the distribution of my mother's jewelry. When I opened the sachet, there was the pendant. The crown jewels would not have been more welcome.

My eyes filled with tears as I looked at it. Tears of joy tinged with sadness and regret that I had not gotten closer to my mother. How stupid we both were to allow convention to stand in the way of our relationships. Either one of us could have bridged the gap but we didn't. No one had taught either of us how to talk about matters of the heart.

When I started my odyssey of transition I was angry that she had not spoken to me about my cross-dressing as a child. Now I am just sad that neither of us knew how to communicate. How much I miss her and wonder what we could have had as mother and daughter.

Later that night the first spring rains started to fall. I sat listening as it fell on my little school house roof. It was one of those deliciously steady falls that you know has settled in for awhile. It was getting late and I enjoyed it as I drifted off to sleep. The sound of rain on a metal roof was the epitome of romance. It drummed steadily and filled the house and my heart with a resonance that calmed my spirit and brought me peace. Many happy memories flooded back to me. Memories from childhood of spring rain on a friend's farmhouse. Winters at Portsea where the rain drove in off the ocean and beat relentlessly on the roof. Storms of unbelievable violence at Wonboyn. Our farm at Officer with the metal roof.

As I sat there with the lights out listening to the steady beat, my cares faded away and warm memories flowed back to me, tearing at my heart and making me wish that my life had been different. My memories also carried a great happiness that far outweighed the sadness.

All that was missing that night was someone with her arms around me, someone to share the joy with.

I originally thought that success meant when I could pass in public and not need to divulge my past to anyone. When I reached the point of being able to pass reasonably well I found that, for me, this was not a practical decision. My new friendships relied more on close confidences and sharing than the ones I had known before. Past friendships had been more social acquaintanceships.

I cherished my new friends and so the act of telling them about my past, while necessary, was frightening because the loss of any one of them would have been a significant blow to me. I realized that in the long run being truthful with the people I cared about was the best route.

With one woman in particular, Nora, I had the beginnings of a strong friendship. After several meetings, dinners and walks I reached a point where I felt the situation could not grow further unless I told her about myself. I couldn't avoid telling details of my past and I did not want to start lying, so I told her everything.

"I knew something was different about you," she said, "but I wasn't sure what. Don't worry. You're a friend."

Nora lived up the road from me and I often spent time with her and helped around the house with feeding the horses or picking blackberries. Her house was on a rise that looked down the valley and we sat on the verandah in the dusk watching woodcocks rise twittering into the evening air and then plunge down in courtship power-dives. Deer and moose walked across the fields below us and black flies swarmed around us, eventually driving us inside to dinner.

As summer approached, I needed to leave my rental, and Nora asked if I wanted to move in with her. I accepted and made plans to move in the first of June. When Nora fell and broke her leg I moved in a week early to help her.

Her support showed me how strong our friendship was. A neighbor who had heard through the grapevine of my change, came to Nora's house one day, out of concern for her, I presumed.

"There's something you should know about that person who is moving in with you," he said.

"I know everything I need to know, thank you. She is very

nice and she is coming to stay," she said with finality.

I emptied the school house and moved out for the next three months. I was sad to leave and arranged to move back in the next winter, when the school house would become a safe haven while I had my operation.

By May my breasts had become much larger, which gave me more confidence. I became conscious of their presence as I moved. If I touched my shoulder they rubbed on my arm. When I reached down to do my toenails they pressed against my leg. Taking a shower took on a whole new dimension as I washed and caressed them and the folds that they created.

I was just short of six months on hormones. In relation to forty-four years of living it was a very short time but during the short period I had lived in the school house my life had been continually in flux.

There was, however, one constant in the whole process. One thing that did not change, except to grow stronger, and that was the conviction that I was doing the right thing. My ideas modified, but not my bottom line. I was a woman.

When I started my change, I had envisioned my final emergence being like the emergence of a butterfly. I expected that, as I grew and changed with the hormones, I would come to resemble the composite woman I had created in my dreams. She would look like a person somewhere between my mother and all the other women I had admired over the years. I waited under my wig until the day when I could take it off and see that person. When I did finally take the wig off I saw that the butterfly had emerged but not as I had expected. I still recognized the old me. I had the same face, the same mind, the same values. I saw, more or less, how I would always look.

What I saw I liked. To me I was beautiful even if the butterfly was not what I had originally expected. I was happy with the outcome. I loved being Jenny. It was a passionate and deep feeling of well being. I felt at last that everything would work out.

On May 19 the AIDS quilt was shown at Dartmouth. I spent the day as a volunteer, making sure no one walked on it as it lay spread across the floor of the gym. It was the most emotional and enlightening thing I had done in a long time. There were over fourteen hundred panels and twelve new ones were added during the three days the quilt was on display. The panels had been made by friends and family of victims and I found it impossible to read more than one or two panels at a time without crying. At the end of the day, after folding up the quilt, I was asked to stay on and join the other volunteers to discuss our feelings and to share the experience with each other.

I wanted to stay but I was also shy. "I have to get home," I murmured and left. Half way home it dawned on me, I did not have to go home, but I did not turn around. It will all be over by the time I get back, I reasoned, and kept on going.

By the beginning of June my electrolysis treatment was up to 46 hours. My cheeks and chin were almost free of coarse hair and I only had my top lip and the last of the side-burns to go. After that my plan was to move down to the vast area of my throat. For some months I had not had to shave my face, other than for my top lip. It was smooth and sensitive to the flow of air. The slightest breeze tickled across it like a feather.

I received the June edition of the XX magazine and the letters and articles referred to the problem of presenting our cause to the general public. Why was it that only the fringe members got interviewed? These people were the most controversial and they did the most for the media's ratings. Many people still saw us as freaks and enjoyed the side show atmosphere that surrounded those who radiated the most stereotypical 'man-in-drag' appearance. A case in point was a person who had fought the medical and legal community to have surgery. Having won, she turned around after surgery and said that it had all been a mistake. The surgery had not made her into a woman.

What many people do not understand is that the surgery does not make any of us into a gender we were not born into. All it does is make us cosmetically acceptable to ourselves and society. It allows us to go unharassed into areas that previously we would have been barred from.

By the middle of June my confidence and self-esteem were increasing. One Saturday in Pat's shop a customer recognized me. I guessed by the way I was being observed. As I wrote up the slip, she said to her friend, "He'll put them in a bag."

The customer was friendly and showed no sign of discomfort. My relaxed attitude had removed any element of threat from the meeting. I was very happy with the way I handled it.

This was not the first customer to notice. Pat had told me that one of her friends had seen me 'as a man.' Two months before I would have retreated into the school house for a week. This time I took no notice and did not get upset.

A question arose about how much time, money, and effort I should devote to my appearance. I wanted to find the line between paranoia about appearance and being comfortable with myself. It was something I was always adjusting. People I had met at the XX club who were transitioning male to female spoke of having tracheal shaves, vocal chord adjustments, cheek bone enhancement, breast implants, buttock enlargement and a shopping list of other cosmetic surgeries. Some treatments like a tracheal shave or vocal chord shortening made life easier for some people. I decided that none of them would make me 'more of a woman,' just more passable, and since I had come to love myself as I was, I saw no need to go further.

Chapter Thirteen

By the end of ten months of electrolysis treatment I only needed to shave my top lip. The hormones had caused a softening of my features. I started to see my mother in my new smooth-skinned face. I also saw some of her mannerisms, how I sat, how I folded my arms and made gestures. The likeness had always been there but now I was looking for it, and was glad when I saw it.

The memory of how I had looked in the past not only affected the way others saw me, it affected my own actions and feelings. I was still vulnerable to being exposed and whenever a reflection of my old self surfaced I tried to change it. Coming home one day I went by Pat's store to browse the new stock and to chat with Danette. I had carefully done my hair, put on some lipstick, and physically looked the same as any other day. The only difference was that I had on blue-jeans and did not feel very feminine. I felt uncomfortably male and wondered if my discomfort showed. I doubt that it did, but I was not comfortable. I was not totally free from John. The person that I had been for forty years still haunted me.

Letters from my father in Australia were full of cutting remarks. I grew sick of writing to him. It was not worth the heartache when he replied. I watched the sun go down and the color drain from the autumn leaves, trying to take in the beauty and displace the sorrow. The color in October 1991 was spectacular. Truen, Laurie's parents' dog, was with me one weekend and I sat and told her all my problems. I came to the conclusion that I had to maintain a connection with my father. I would have to tolerate the anguish in his letters in the hope that sometime in the future he would come to accept the new me. I escaped from these belittling tirades by filling my life with new pursuits.

I took some college courses because I wanted to learn new skills and because I saw it as a way to meet people and develop new friendships.

In the past I had hidden in the middle of a social group. When I started taking courses it was very different. Not only was I taking classes that interested me, but I was no longer trying to hide; I could participate without fear of being discovered as 'queer' or 'perverted,' so I allowed myself to excel. I got an A, or its equivalent, for every course I took.

The first course was a psychology course at Community College of Vermont. For the first time I was enjoying going to classes. It was only an introductory class but I was learning a lot and intended to go on and take other classes.

One of the first papers I wrote was on gender bias against women in the mental health profession. It was interesting to research and set me to thinking. Did I have the right to speak for women? Was my vicarious experience good enough? Was I being presumptuous in thinking I knew about gender discrimination, when for so long I had sat on the other side of the fence? Would other women feel slighted when I gave my views, or was the fact that I was from 'the other side' be a strength? I had been trained in the ways of men. I had been included in their conspiracies and had tried, in many ways, to emulate them. I think that I was scared of someone saying "you don't have the right."

But I gave my report and it was well received, despite my nervousness.

My social contacts at college and the local lesbian community proved to be excellent networks. Socially, though, I felt that some people in the lesbian community didn't see me as female, and therefore considered me an interloper and not really a lesbian. There were only a few, but even so I was somewhat surprised. Although I did not agree with them, I believed that it was their prerogative to feel that way, even though it seemed unjust to discriminate against me for nothing more than the way I had been socialized. I did not have their many years of female socialization but I did feel I had a right to have my input on women's affairs as they affected me, and to have these views heard as coming from a woman.

Conversely, as a transgendered person, I did not feel I could demand to be a part of any social or political lesbian group that unanimously wanted to exclude me. I felt that each group had the right to set and maintain its own standards, as long as these standards were legal and openly expressed.

I did, however, feel it was a shame that so many women in lesbian separatist groups excluded transgendered people on the grounds that they were really men. To me this showed a total ignorance of what it meant to be a transgendered person of either sex. Their definition of a woman was limited to 'womyn-born-womyn,' so even a person who underwent gender assignment surgery soon after birth would be excluded. I may have been categorized as male at birth, but I was certainly not then, nor have I ever been, a male.

Despite how happy I was feeling and how successfully I was assimilating back into the general community, elements of deep depression still lingered. One morning I was lying in bed, feeling warm and comfortable, still drowsy, when I started thinking how a bottle of sleeping pills could maintain this euphoria indefinitely. No major crisis had occurred, and yet it took the better part of the day until I gave up my feelings.

I thought perhaps it had occurred because Christmas was approaching and I had mixed emotions about it. The joy of watching Sam open presents and listening to carols I remembered from my childhood conflicted with the fact that I had only received two Christmas cards from Australia.

But good things were happening. My best Christmas present that year came from Laurie. I had gone to Montreal on December

10 to meet with a doctor and arrange for surgery. When I told Laurie that I had set a date of March 2 she said that she wanted to come up and be with me when I came out of surgery. What a shame, I thought, that she is not even just a little bit a lesbian.

While in Montreal a heavy snow storm had made it impossible for me to return to Strafford after my appointment with the doctor. In the waiting room I had been talking to a pre-operative black woman who was a professional model and dancer working in Canada and Germany. I was jealous of her youth and beauty and saw in her what I could have been if only I had been able to make the change in my teens or earlier. She told me about Sarah, a post-operative transgendered woman who had an apartment where she boarded people during recuperation from the operation. I rang her to see if I could get a room for the night.

For an hour or so after putting down a deposit for the operation I had the feeling that I had just committed myself to more than I could financially afford. When I saw Sarah's apartment, I really wondered if I was doing the right thing. The place wasn't anything special but Sarah had experience that could save me from accidentally damaging myself as I healed. I stayed there that night and then arranged to board there after surgery.

After that experience I felt I knew something about how a woman feels when she is arranging an abortion. First I had had to lie to the Canadian border guards and tell them I was on a pleasure trip. Then I had to go to a basement waiting room of a foreign doctor and pay a five hundred dollar deposit, in cash, to a stranger. This was followed by a night in an apartment owned by a heavy smoker in pink sweats. I felt that the sooner it was over the happier I would be. I still knew I was doing the right thing.

I started counting. The surgery I had waited a lifetime for was now only sixty-seven days away. The doctor seemed nice. He was currently doing two gender reassignment operations every week. The length of time since my first visit to Hartford seemed to have flown by and dragged on, both at the same time. I had achieved a lot, yet I still had a long way to go. The medication was doing its job, and I was working part-time, taking college courses and doing volunteer work. My list of friends was growing and life had established a degree of normalcy.

Some things still needed to be attended to though. Before surgery I had to be divorced. No surgeon, I found, would operate if I was married. They didn't want to be held libel if my wife sued for 'loss of conjugal rights.'

When I got back from Montreal I found a full-time job working with United Developmental Services, an agency that supported people living with a disability. My job was to help people find a job and then assist them in their integration into the workplace. They were empathetic towards me and very supportive. They employed me even after one of my references, the owner of the farm I had been working on, 'outed' me when they called to check my references.

I enjoyed the job and came to deeply respect the clients I worked with. Despite sometimes having severe mental disabilities they all had developed wonderful ways of coping with life. I learned that a touch on the knee can mean more than a hug, and that streams of abuse need not mean "I hate you." Their thrill at being able to fasten a seat belt could be as great for them as any of my 'A' grades was for me—and that it could make me feel just as good.

I also saw, over and over, how cruel and intolerant many people were towards anyone they considered disabled or different. Someone had the gall to approach us in the street and say, "These animals should not be allowed out in public." It infuriates me to realize that there are people in our society who think like this, and worse, are unashamed to voice their bigotry in public.

Some of the clients I worked with were employed at a local grocery store. It was a place that I shopped at and some of the staff knew about my change-over. When I started going there with the clients, I met my own kind of discrimination. Evidently someone in the store complained to UDS that I should not be working with disabled people. They felt I was a threat to them. I had to defend myself again, but the people at UDS were wonderfully supportive. If I had been laid off, I would have had no recourse, since transgenderism was not covered by anti-discrimination laws.

I got depressed when I thought about how many times I had had to justify myself. But I still knew that I was doing the right thing and that nothing would ever make me go back to where I had come from.

I met Lisa, a co-worker, through UDS and we became firm friends. It took me a while to be honest about myself. I still hoped that one day I would be able to stop telling people about my past. I feared that when she, and others, found out they would no longer like me. After I told her, however, our friendship strengthened and we spent many wonderful hours together.

The town I lived in, Strafford, Vermont, was the home of William Sloane-Coffin, a well-known minister and peace activist since the 1960s. I never got to know him closely but my friend Nora was his secretary. Quite often when I was staying with her he would come up to the house and we would talk. Later I heard from Nora that he had supported me in the community more than once. One of his friends, the playwright Arthur Miller, stayed in Strafford for a week or so each summer. On a summer evening it was wonderful to walk to the old town meeting house and listen to him read. On one visit to Nora's house, William Sloane-Coffin gave me a quote which I still cherish: "To survive is important but to thrive is elegant." It was from the writings of Maya Angelou, he said.

It is quite normal for relatives of transgendered people to feel that the person they knew before had died and been replaced by someone else. The feeling is so deep that they literally go through a period of mourning for that person before they can accept the new one. Some of my own friends and family honestly said that this was how they felt about my change.

As if to reinforce the sense of loss, Christmas mail and photos that year were sent to Laurie, as if I no longer existed. I had heard horror stories like this from the gay and lesbian community and from other transgendered people but I never thought it would happen to me.

In February I went to a seminar by a Dr. Shaefer, who at seventy-two years old was an articulate and eloquent speaker and the President of the Harry Benjamin International Gender Dysphoria Association. Dr. Shaefer referred to many of the feelings I was having. She explained that the treatment I was receiving from my Australian family and others was normal and not specific to me. She had worked with gender issues since 1975 and had counselled, by her count, more than four hundred and fifty transgendered and transvestite clients over the years.

She believed that transgenderism occurred because of a failure of the physical sex to be correctly aligned to the brain in the period before birth when the fetus, which is initially female, takes on the specific sexual features which makes it appear male or female. She believed that there was no cure, psychological or medical, for this misalignment, and that a person should be allowed, through hormone treatment and surgery, to adjust one's lifestyle to meet one's current needs.

People came to the final step of surgery at different times in their lives. Dr. Shaefer had worked with a sixty-seven year old person who had lived openly as a woman for twenty years without surgery. At this late date, she had chosen surgery only to avoid having a male body in her grave.

Dr. Shaefer talked of confronting a person's feelings of guilt. She called it "existential guilt for an existential crime." Very early in life, she explained, a child feels that she or he is different. They do not know the reason for the difference but they begin to feel guilty for not being the same as other people, and they begin to blame themselves. This belief leads to a string of self-destructive actions as they try to deny their feelings. They continually try to be the perfect representative of their apparent gender, going to extremes to hide their true self.

As Dr. Shaefer talked, I looked around at the audience. I saw many people who would never be able to pass as women without large amounts of cosmetic surgery, and maybe not even then. Until that afternoon I had had a subconscious feeling that one had to look like a woman to be one, that people who obviously did not 'pass' should not go out in public, that they were masquerading as women. I felt this way because I was scared of being ridiculed myself and was threatened by these 'masculine-looking women.' It was as if I could see myself in them. They were all I was trying to get away from. By the end of the meeting, I felt differently about them.

I came away from the meeting feeling that people who are not transgendered often do not want to discuss the topic because it causes them to rethink their own gender. Transgendered people show them that what they previously had thought immutable can actually be changed. And worse, that we reject the gender proclamation made at our births.

I also came away feeling angry. Why was I discriminated against? If I lived with muscular dystrophy or another socially acceptable condition, I would be respected and showered with financial support to help me change. As it was I was more likely to become penniless and be shunned by society and humiliated in the hospitals.

Chapter Fourteen

In early February 1992 I went to court and, with the help of my lawyer who had arranged for me to see the most tolerant judge, I got my divorce. Everything went smoothly and I felt no different after it than I had before. All it did was legalize what had been a reality for the last two years.

The only thing of note was the look on the young court recorder's face at the end of the hearing when she realized that I was not born a woman. Her mouth hung open as she stared. I smiled and said "thank you" but her expression remained unchanged. She had either never met a transgendered person before, or my existence had unwittingly told her something about a friend, or herself.

The management at UDS remained supportive and I arranged for three weeks off without pay for my operation and recuperation. Keeping it a secret from my co-workers was hard because I was so happy. I wanted to tell everyone. I wanted to share my happiness with the world.

I knew that this operation was important. I finally would have a body that was aesthetically acceptable to me. As it was, I felt incomplete. No one could see, under normal circumstances, the anatomical incongruity, yet for my own contentment I need-ed to make the final adjustment. I wanted to stand naked before the world and say, "See you were wrong! I am a woman."

All my life I had feared that I would suffer some accidental unmasking. I had feared being branded a 'poofter' at school. Later I feared I would be humiliated in public by a pair of torn pants or hospitalization after an accident. I lived in fear that someone would see women's clothes on a man. Someone would sense the confusion of my whole life. But after the operation no one would ever again see a penis on the woman that I was. At last I would not have to live with the fear of being accidentally unmasked.

One fear returned though. The fear was that I would die before I got through the operation. As I waited impatiently for surgery I feared that something would happen. Was I irrational? Maybe. But it felt real. It was a very long two weeks.

A week before my scheduled surgery my emotional state was agitated. I found it hard to sleep. In the evening I danced around my house and sang and hugged myself. I felt as though I was about to embark on the trip of a lifetime, a dream trip where I knew that all my expectations were about to be fulfilled.

I was asked during that week to put my feelings into words and the best I could do was: Imagine that you are about to leave on an all-expense paid trip with the person of your dreams. You will be visiting every exotic place you have ever wanted to see and there is absolutely no time or expense limit. Emotionally I was in seventh heaven. I was floating on air.

I smiled a lot that week and counted the moments until I would awake after the operation. I had never awaited anything in my life with such eager anticipation.

To help control myself I kept busy. I had two visits to the electrolysist, an appointment with Betty, and a college class. I also had to pick up money and finish shopping for the essentials I would need.

I had told Betty about my fear of dying before the operation, even though I knew it was irrational. She wanted to know if I was nervous about dying under the anesthetic or losing my penis. I smiled and assured her that I felt fine, but that if anything stopped me from getting the surgery then she would have a real basket case on her hands.

Two days later I got home from work and there was a message on my answering machine to call the doctor's secretary in

Montreal. There was nothing I could do until the next morning, Thursday, and all night I was convinced that there was some sort of hitch, that everything would be delayed, or worse, canceled. But when I called she just wanted to give me directions to the clinic.

On Friday night, Laurie, Sam and I went to dinner at Laurie's parents. It was a fun night with steaks on the grill and a bottle of Australian Seaview Shiraz. The night was capped by Fred taking my wrists, looking me in the eyes, and saying that if I needed anything while I was in Montreal, I was to call him.

All I could do was give him a hug and say thank you. Marje also gave me an Australian-designed Ken Donne sponge bag to take with me. It was certainly better than the plastic bread bag that I had been using up until then.

On Saturday morning I packed the car and made sure I had everything. I saw Nora and then walked back down the snow-lined road, watching chickadees and nuthatches as they searched in the bare trees for food.

After dinner I drew myself a hot bath and shaved. I had to remove all my pubic hair before the operation and I wanted to do it in the privacy of my own home, rather than in the shared bath-room of the hospital.

On Sunday, March 1, Laurie and I set out for Montreal. It was a quiet trip. I thought about what I was about to do, and worried about the car breaking down on the way to the clinic. All went smoothly, though.

We stopped at the Canadian border check and they asked to see my green card. "What is the purpose of the visit?" he asked.

"Just pleasure," I said. "I will be in Canada for about two weeks."

"Where are you staying?"

"With a friend in Laval," I said, hoping that my lie was not showing.

When we arrived in Montreal Laurie checked into the hotel where she was going to stay for the night and we went for a walk

149

around town. It was a cold, overcast day so we drifted aimlessly from shop to shop, trying to kill time. Because the operation was the next day, I couldn't even eat a good meal.

Check-in time was 6 p.m. I was scared of being late so we arrived fifteen minutes early to find the place closed. It was a small clinic that mainly performed cosmetic surgery on women from Sunday evening until Friday night. I did not know this at the time and so we sat and waited until a nurse arrived and unlocked the door.

The admitting procedures were standard, except that I had to hand over full payment, in advance. I was shown to my room and then Laurie gave me a kiss and left me to wait the last few hours.

After she left I was alone except for the admitting nurse. It sounded like the operation would not be until late the next morning or early afternoon. I had only eaten a sandwich for lunch. Soon I would be starving. I dreaded the delay.

I was told that a woman from Oakland, California, was also being admitted that night. I assumed she was having the same operation. I was glad I didn't have to travel so far.

Alone and hungry in the room I had the fleeting thought, "Why am I doing this?" Making plans when I was safe at home and three hours from the hospital was easy. Waiting in a hospital bed was another matter. I realized that from that moment on there was no going back. It was forever.

The bed covering was a cotton sheet and a thin cotton blanket and I was getting cold. I considered calling the nurse and asking for another one but I did not want to disturb her. I looked at the other bed and its blanket but left it there because the other patient would be arriving shortly. My flannel nightie helped a bit, so I just curled up and waited.

The worst thing was that all the staff knew why I was there. I felt as though, again, I was 'the man dressed as a woman.' At 9:15 p.m. I was still awake; cold and lonely.

Forty-five minutes later I was still lying in bed with the light on, not wanting to go to sleep before my roommate arrived. I wondered if she would be divine like the woman I had met in the waiting room. As long as she was not nosy, I thought, I could put up with a lot. But if she was one of those people who talked all the time it would be a long week. I decided if in an hour she hadn't arrived I would go to sleep. At 11 p.m. I turned out the light and hugged my knees to my chest.

When I woke the next morning I was still alone. I could not have breakfast but the worst of my hunger was gone. Mid-morning the nurse came in and started getting me ready for the operation. After the first calming needle she left me alone. About half an hour later they wheeled me to the operating room, which turned out to be on the second floor, right above my room.

I lay waiting in an anteroom until someone having a face lift was wheeled out and parked next to me. Then it was my turn. The last thing I did was smile at the anesthetist and say something that was supposed to sound light-hearted. Then I drifted off to sleep. I did not wake up until 10 a.m. Tuesday morning, twenty-four hours later.

I was flat on my back and a little sore. The most amazing thing was that, although my penis was gone, I felt as though nothing was missing. I had imagined before the operation that I would look down and say to myself, "Doesn't it look great, now that it's gone." I had no feelings of loss. Rationally I could see I had changed, but emotionally I felt I was just as I should be.

My roommate still had not arrived. Most of the day I dozed and in the afternoon the doctor came in, took a quick look, and said with a broad French accent, "Good, very good. Do you have any pain? No? I will leave pain killers for you if you need them."

That night I had a meal of beautifully cooked fish. The woman who brought it asked in accented English what I wanted for breakfast, as though I was in a Montreal hotel. It turned out that I was the only patient staying over night. Everyone else was having day surgery. The only person the kitchen was cooking for was me.

On Wednesday morning I got out of bed and tried sitting in a chair. I had had a good sleep but had woken at three and then drifted in and out of sleep. I had not needed any pain killers, not even an aspirin.

Emotionally I was calm. I had done what was needed and could now continue my life. I was a woman who had needed some corrective surgery. The growth was gone and my labia, clitoris and vagina were free. It was done. I felt no deeper, emotionally, than that.

By Thursday afternoon I was bored silly. I felt great and just wanted to go home. I was sick of sitting around draining my bladder into a bag and reading or watching awful daytime television.

I filled my time by walking around looking at the clinic. It was built in the northern suburbs of Montreal and had a view across park land to the Ottawa River. From the outside the building was severe and uninviting. It was a two-story rectangle built next to the road with no grounds or landscaping. Inside it was new and modern with rooms opening off a central reception area. The surgery was all done on the second floor, over my head, and I often heard people being wheeled in and out. I had not seen any other patient while I was there and because of the design of the building I basically had a private suite.

The sensation of being complete remained with me. Most of the bandages were taken off on Thursday morning and I looked down to see that everything was as it should be. I was pleased.

A couple of times I felt physically what I would have called an erection. There was a tightening in the area of my new vagina and clitoris and I decided that if this was an indication of how sex would one day feel then I may end up a nymphomaniac.

After leaving the hospital I had arranged to stay on in Montreal with Sarah for a week. For a small charge she provided board, post-op care and guidance on how to look after my new vagina. It was not the most comfortable arrangement. The flat was small and since it was winter we had to keep the windows closed and the air was thick and stuffy. I opened the window in my bedroom just a little each night so I could feel the coolness and get some fresh air.

Sarah was a chain smoker. She also stayed awake all night watching television. The constant background noise of sitcoms and soaps from across the hall droned on until I fell asleep. It woke me again the next morning. Sarah and her partner were, however, very kind. They had helped many other post-op women, and they knew exactly how to carry out the dilating and douching that I had to do five times a day for the first six weeks. Without them it would have been extremely difficult for me.

Sarah also told me about the woman who was supposed to have shared a room with me. She had had the operation some two months earlier, and had taken a hotel room alone in Montreal for the week, until the packing could be removed from her new vagina. She then flew straight home. She had not learned how to use the stint (a nylon dildo-type instrument) properly and was using it too forcefully because she wanted to have sex with her boyfriend as soon as possible. As a result she had forced the stint into her rectum and the vagina had become infected.

She had had the damage repaired in California but now she was returning to have the vagina reconstructed. For some reason she had become scared and after arriving in the Montreal airport she had called the night nurse to cancel her appointment. She caught the next plane back to California.

Sarah said others, finding that they could not go through with the surgery, had also canceled late. I was told about someone who had entered the clinic, spent the night, and then left the next morning before surgery. Late changes of mind were not common. The twelve month transition period usually gave people plenty of time to decide if what they were doing was the right thing for them or not.

Dilating was the most important part of the care program. The walls of the vagina had to be kept separated so that they did not heal together. To stop this from happening the surgeon had sewn a condom packed with cotton wool into the vagina. It stayed there for the first week, until he removed the stitches and took it out.

After this I was provided with a nylon stint that I was to insert and use in a manner similar to a dildo for fifteen minutes every three hours for the next six weeks. This stretched the inverted penal skin that formed the walls of my vagina. It also kept the walls separated. Initially I did not enjoy using the stint. As soon as I was back home in Strafford I became less and less diligent about the procedure.

One reason was that I really never expected that anyone would love me enough to accept me sexually, and therefore I felt I had no need of a vagina. Once the swelling had gone down a little, though, my ideas changed because my newly constructed clitoris quickly came to life. What had been a chore suddenly became a new and very exciting experience. I found that with changes and variations in speed and rotation of the stint or dildo, I could achieve the most wonderful sexual sensations. One night, about three weeks after returning home, I had an orgasm, and this ensured my continued diligent use of the stint.

When I went back to work I was supposed to be using the stint for fifteen minutes every three hours. To do this I laid half naked on the tile floor of the bathroom using my coat as a rug. It was uncomfortable and in three weeks I had given up using the stint during the day and resigned myself to only using it each morning and evening.

The only difficulty I had with the whole operation was learning to urinate again. I no longer instinctively knew which muscles to relax. I had to sit and concentrate on my urethra for some time before I got the right ones to let go. Also, for a few months I reached down to aim my now nonexistent penis into the bowl. Years of habit die slowly.

These were really the only two inconveniences that I suffered from the whole operation. I had had no pain and only a small amount of discomfort when I first started using the stint. I had been warned to expect intense pain and discomfort for the first six weeks and I felt very lucky. The reason for my lack of pain may have been that I was totally relaxed about having the operation. I had no fears or doubts. After all, I was just going in to have some 'cosmetic surgery to remove a non-malignant growth that was blocking the entrance to my vagina.' What was there to worry about?

After the surgery I no longer needed to carry my security letter from the Hartford support group. While still physically a man, this letter had given me legal protection to be in public dressed as a woman. In many states it was illegal for a man to dress as a woman in public, and in most it was illegal for a man to go into a women-only toilet.

Dr. Higgins had signed the letter on November 20, 1990, and now, just fifteen months later, it was superfluous. It had been just twenty-five months since I had last visited Australia and just eighteen months since I had moved into the school house.

The only ongoing task left for me now was to slowly try and rebuild my connections with my family in Australia. I wanted to go back, although I was not sure how this would turn out. At Easter, seven weeks after the operation, I was reminded by an intolerant letter from Australia how hard it really was going to be.

Chapter Fifteen

Summer was coming and it was time to find somewhere to live again. Nora offered her room but I wanted to find somewhere more permanent. The school house had been perfect for my transition but now I needed to plan for the long term. I needed somewhere I could start rebuilding my life and settling down.

I mentioned this to Pat and she suggested the apartment over her store in South Strafford. There was a student in it at the time but she was leaving at the end of June. The apartment was next door to the general store and the porch outside the kitchen looked into the treetops and down onto the Ompompanoosuc River. At that point it was little more than a brook but it riffled over rock and I could hear its gentle burbling through the screened-in porch. Moving in there meant I needed to find a place to live for a month but the inconvenience was worth it.

I asked around and found a room for a month. It wasn't perfect but I took it and moved in. Afterwards I found out that my new landlady was a teacher at Sam's school. I was faced with another predicament. Because so many people around town knew about my change, including some of the teachers at the school, I felt I should tell her and try and make her comfortable having me in the house. This was one of my worst misjudgments of character. Instead of being understanding, she became distant without actually being rude or moving. I spent most of that month either reading in my room or away from the house.

By the end of June I was desperate. The move to Pat's was looking better every day.

On the first of July I loaded everything I owned into my car and drove the few kilometers to my new apartment. It was a warm summer day and my heart was singing. I was out of the rented room and had once more landed on my feet. I was about to move into a beautiful apartment all to myself. Not only was it nearly as romantic as the school house, but it was larger, and gave Sam his own room.

I arrived with all my dreams floating around me in the sunlight and read the note that was on the door. It said that the current tenant had decided not to move out and that I could not have the apartment. I knew it wasn't Pat's fault. She had done everything she could to help but I was devastated. I had moved out of my rented room and had nowhere else to go.

I went back to my car and cried my eyes out until the shock had declined and I started to think again. It seemed that my only option was to go back to Laurie and see if I could sleep on the futon in the loft until I found somewhere else to live. I drove over and told her, between sobs, what had happened and she kindly said I could stay for awhile.

The next day I drove down to Dartmouth and picked up a copy of the housing vacancy list. There was very little available but one place sounded reasonable, although it was considerably outside the area that I preferred to live in. I called the number and arranged to go over and see it that evening.

The house was at the end of one and a half miles of rough, steep road on top of a hill. As I drove up through the trees I felt that it was silly to even contemplate living at the end of such a bad road, but then the trees started to thin and I emerged into a large field, at the top of which was the house. As soon as I saw it I knew I would like it. Deb, the owner, was working in the garden when I got there and we went inside to look at the room she had available.

My relationship with Deb turned out to be one of those friendships that work from the first moment. We sat around for about two hours drinking wine and coffee, talking about our likes and dislikes, comparing our dreams and desires. By the time I left I felt as though I had known her forever. I moved in the next weekend.

The other person renting a room in the house was a law student named Kevin. I was dubious about sharing with a man at first but he turned out to be a very kind and thoughtful person. We often went for walks together and he was more social than either Deb or I so if there was a dinner party or barbecue at the house, it was likely that he had arranged it with friends from the law school.

From the back door of the house I could walk or ski old town roads back into the woods for many kilometers. In Fall the view south over the valley of the White River was superb. The leaves turned so many colors of red and gold, burgundy and yellow, that even photos do not do it justice. In the winter everything turned black and white, as snow covered the ground and bare branches swung and crackled in the sub-zero air.

In spring the road to the house turned into a river of mud. It was often necessary to park at the bottom of the hill and walk to the house. With the return of warm weather, buds started to swell on the trees and steam rose from the sugaring sheds as they reduced forty gallons of maple sap to one gallon of pure syrup. Birds arrived on the southerly winds, heralding their arrival with an unaccustomed soft twittering high in the branches, or from some grass or shrub barely free from the last of the snow. First to arrive were the blackbirds, and their call of "O-Kar-Eee" was often subliminal for some time before it rose from the subconscious to the conscious and I realized that the birds were back from their wintering grounds in the southern states.

From the picture windows of Deb's hilltop house I also witnessed the passing of a plethora of weather formations. Snow storms rolled white over the valleys and rain came in heavy squalls with a front line that cut the sky, top to bottom, between blue and black, as cleanly as a scimitar. Fog lay so still and dense in the valley that I expected to see polar bears appear as if walking on a snow-covered tundra. Lightning struck the hills, lighting the sky as if it were day.

One evening there was a display of natural beauty so subtle and gracious that it was mesmerizing. The southern horizon was aglow with an ethereal, slowly evolving spectrum of sunlight on clouds.

The sky to the east was a soft blue, the color of Delft pottery. It faded to the palest aquamarine in the south, before flaring to flame pink at the western horizon.

High up in the east were wisps of soft-pink cloud, the color of the softest rose in the garden. To the west the setting sun turned the long lenticular clouds that marched up like waves from the horizon a dark slate-gray. One small cloud was stark white like a crescent moon, except at its lower end. Here it fanned like a feather and was the color of the crest on a Major Mitchell cockatoo, all pinks and whites and every shade between. So many soft colors were laid on one small cloud so small you could hide it with your hand.

The display unfolded with slow majesty. The milk-white between the western clouds slowly evolved to a pale blue-green, the color of a coral sea. Along the horizon, below the clouds, it turned to the soft pink of a guava, before sunset eventually stole the last of the color and all went dark.

During my time at Deb's I fell in love. It was a whirlwind affair that only lasted two months. We met at dinner at a mutual friend's one night and she rang me up and invited me out the next evening. For the next two months I spent every moment I could with her. I was floating. I even considered staying on in America forever. I told her that I was transgendered and she said that it was okay, she loved me anyway.

We went to restaurants, films and down to New York to see a Matisse exhibition. During the Fall we walked for miles and talked and read. Unfortunately she was also suffering from an illness and much of our time together was spent in doctors' waiting rooms.

Then one day before Christmas, without any warning, she told me it was over. She gave no reason or explanation. She just said our relationship was finished and she never wanted to see me again. I collapsed in tears and wandered out to my car. When I got home I telephoned but there was no answer. I left messages on her machine. I went back to her house but she wasn't there. Eventually she called me and told me I was being silly.

A day or two later, after I had finally calmed down, I felt that my belief that I was sexually unlovable had been confirmed. I was resigned to spending the rest of my life with friends, but living sexually alone.

The season was further tainted by another incident of harassment. One night after dinner with the friend of some friends, I was invited by my host to go out and look at a feature of his barn. We had been talking about barn building and design. He got a flashlight and we went out through the snow into the old building. He took me over to one of the stalls and shone the beam up into rafters. Then he moved hard up against me and put his head near my cheek. He asked if I could see a specific joint. I pushed away and said, "Yes, thank you very much," and hurried back to the house ahead of him. I sat down at the table and he soon came in. The air between us was as cold as the night outside but I felt I could not say anything out of courtesy to his wife, my hostess.

When my ability to pass had been more questionable I had felt obliged to tell people about myself very early on in a friendship so as to avoid an unexpected "outing." I lacked confidence in myself and wanted to remove some of the possible complications from my life. The first friend who I confided in was Nora. In those early days it was necessary. Close up I was not very convincing to any observant person. The next person was Pat and I told her because I was going to be working in her store and I knew that there would be customers who would know fairly quickly that I was transgendered. After that I told other co-workers in order to share a more intimate relationship. The last person I told was the person I rented the room from for a month. When I left that house I moved in with Deb and Kevin, and I had to decide again whether or not to tell them. Because of that last experience, I decided not to.

As the months went by and we became close friends I sometimes wished that I had told them about myself in the beginning. My fear now became that one of them would find out and be insulted by my secrecy and I would lose their friendship.

Against this fear I weighed the pleasure of living wholly as a woman. Because of my first girlfriend, I knew that the fear of losing a friendship was not unreasonable. My only consolation was that I had told her from the very beginning, and I still lost her friendship and the relationship.

This was the quandary that life presented me. To tell or not to tell. It was an ongoing question, the answer to which would change as my life evolved.

The resolve not to tell Deb and Kevin soon changed as our friendship strengthened. I picked a time with each of them and filled them in on my past. They were both wonderfully supportive and, as had often happened in the past, it helped our friendship move on to new levels. I was learning that, for me, a friendship could go only so far before I had to tell a person about my past. It was too much of who I was to leave it out. I was proud of what I had achieved and I loved Sam and Laurie and all the others who had supported them. As long as it didn't injury anyone, I was going to be honest.

During the time I lived with Deb and Kevin I also started seriously writing poetry. Up until then I had only done it as a means of expressing some thoughts that did not seem to fit into my diary or other prose writings. I started a poetry course and got some compliments about my writing from Pam, the teacher.

After six classes she wrote a comment on one of my poems that said it was good but that she felt I was hiding something and that my poetry would never improve until I was prepared to write from the heart. I must allow myself to explore all my emotions freely. I made an appointment to see her and said that I knew what she meant, but that she would need to know a lot more about me before I could submit such poems for her comments.

161

She said that she was prepared to listen, so I told her about my being transgendered and showed her some poems that gave her an indication of the type of things I wanted to write about. This led to my writing two sets of poetry, one set that could be submitted openly to the class for criticism, and another that only Pam saw.

After the class finished I approached her about doing an independent study with me. She agreed and the end result, after three months of concentrated writing, was a collection of over sixty poems. It was an incredible experience to write so steadily over such a short time. I often got up at six or seven in the morning, and would still be writing at two the next morning.

Chapter Sixteen

In January 1993 I had a tremendous urge to visit Australia. I wanted to run back to my birth home. It was not something that happened overnight, but something that built slowly over time until one day I knew that it had arrived. Somewhere in the rush of Christmas preparations I called my sister, Mandy. My spirit was in full-fledged flight toward those eucalyptus covered hills and that slow drawl—and nothing but landing in Melbourne and smelling that special air would quench my need. I could not really afford to go and I knew that the initial welcome from my family might well be strained, to say the least, but I had to go.

I knew that I had made a lot of mistakes during my visit in 1990. I had inflicted more pain than I had expected or wanted. It had been the first move that I had knowingly taken on my long voyage of discovery and I hadn't realized the incredible repercussions—on both sides of the world. At the time I was excited that I had found the courage I needed to talk about who I was and I expected that everyone would be as excited and happy as I was. On my next trip, I planned to be more considerate of others than I had been on my first trip.

Despite my emotional expectations, I was really looking forward to just being in Australia. I was desperate to hear a Currawong, a Galah, a Willie Wagtail. I wanted to walk in the bush and inhale the scents of my past. I wanted to sit and dream of things, past and future. I wanted to watch the sun rise over the Kulkyne, and go down over Wonboyn Lake. I wanted to see trams and trains, and cars on the 'right' side of the road. Most of all I wanted to go home. With my new found emotions I had developed a need for being part of my family. I hoped that they wanted to be a part of me too.

By March I couldn't wait any longer. I wanted to take Sam, but I didn't know if I should. It would be the first time that the family had ever seen me as Jennifer and I didn't know what their reaction would be.

I went to the travel agent and found that if I waited until early June I would be able to get discount tickets. It would be a struggle to wait that long but the discount was worth it, especially if it meant that Sam could come. I spoke to Laurie and her sister Barb about taking Sam. Laurie was not sure what to do but Barb said she felt he should go. We decided to ask Sam and he was ecstatic. He said he had wanted to come but he didn't think he would be allowed. I explained that I did not know how I would be received when we arrived, but he still said that he wanted to come and was not worried.

I wrote and told people that Sam and I would be coming and asked if we could stay with them. My father said yes, as did Mandy, but I sensed some anger in her letter and I felt she was expressing some of her fears and frustrations with me and with what I was doing.

I called her on the phone about her letter and she said that I was just being selfish in coming, only looking for support from my family. She believed that the visit would not achieve anything apart from disruption and pain. I agreed that it could be disruptive but said that I was the same person I had always had been, I just looked different. I wanted them to see me and hopefully lose some of their fears about who I had become.

By the end of the call we at least knew more about each other and how we felt about my visit. It was one of the first times that we had seriously talked about anything. Even though it was very hard I wished it had happened more often.

In the weeks leading up to the flight I had very mixed feelings about leaving Vermont in the spring. I realized that when the time came for me to leave permanently I would be very sad.

There were also practical things to consider. On my arrival, should I look androgynous in my blue-jeans and a shirt or should I wear a dress, and make the statement that I was now really a woman? How should I greet people, with a handshake or a hug and a kiss? I finally settled on a loose blue denim skirt and a purple and plum checked shirt that would be easy to travel in, and hopefully not too confronting. I could not decide between the handshake and the hug so I decided to do what felt comfortable at the time.

Laurie drove us down to Logan Airport in Boston where she planned to meet Brian, her latest boyfriend, and then drive back to Gove Hill with him. I was calm about going but also apprehensive about how I would be accepted. My father was collecting us from the airport and we would be staying with him for a few nights.

The flight to Australia went as quickly as any long flight can. I was still writing poetry and I spent the time writing and watching the on-flight movies with Sam. We spoke a bit about what we were expecting and what Sam remembered of Australia. He had been four when we left so I was not sure if he would remember anything.

The flight came straight into Melbourne and after going through Customs we looked around the crowded arrival hall for my father. We saw him standing by one of the doors looking our way, but at some point behind us. I smiled and waved and he looked startled when he saw me.

I said, "Hi Dad."

His first words to me were, "You look just like your sister Mandy."

Hugs did not seem appropriate, but they never had been with him, so the three of us just said hello and we walked in the direction of his car.

That afternoon a friend of my father's, Bev, came over to say hello and obviously to give him some moral support. It was the first time we had met and she welcomed Sam and me warmly. After she left we went over to my aunt's for dinner and had a

165

pleasant evening despite the continual flow of incorrect pronouns. Both she and my father calling me John. This was something I had expected and I had decided not to worry about correcting people. I knew that old habits were hard to break, especially after forty-three years. As we were leaving my aunt said to me, "Just relax." I had not realized that I was nervous, but I must have been.

One thing I noticed early on was that my father had trouble looking at me. As we talked he looked out the window, or at the blank television screen, anywhere but at me.

For the first few days we toured around Melbourne as he did his shopping. He took us to old haunts to see what changes had taken place. We went to Sam's old kindergarten in Narre Warren. It was one of the few places that he remembered, and he ran around pointing at things and telling us what had happened to whom and when. Then we went to see my Mother's grave, something that I had never done, despite the fact that she had died over fourteen years before. I had only recently been able to mourn her death, and I could not accept that she was beneath that small metal plate. I preferred to imagine her walking free in her beloved outback.

The next person we visited was my sister Mandy in Warrnambool. I rented a car for the four hour drive and Sam and I headed west from Melbourne. Warrnambool is on the coast but to get there it was necessary to drive out across the flat basalt plains of Victoria's Western District, with its large sheep farms and small country towns.

I loved those plains and their old red gums with their massive, gnarled and twisted limbs reaching out and up to the sparse olive-colored leaves that clustered raggedly at their ends. The flatness of the land let my vision travel for miles, ending in a tremble of heat haze, out of which the trees and hills came and went with my imagination. The sheep appeared to walk on mirages, indistinct, two feet above the dirt of their paddocks.

The air was so clear that I could see wedge-tailed eagles, with their six-foot wing span spiral above me, so high they seemed no larger than the little bush-flies that hung in a sticky mist around my face and back. After having been away from the country for so long I welcomed even those annoying little bush-flies in their millions. They were one of those things that made Australia feel like home to me.

When we reached Warrnambool the welcome was cordial but forced. Mandy was friendly enough, but I sensed that she was troubled having me in the house. The closest she came to voicing what was wrong was when she said that if I made a noise, like a cough when I was not in the room, she expected to see John walk through the door.

After that I started to pick up small signs that showed the general discomfort I was causing. Since I had arrived no one had said they were glad to see me. No one had commented on how I looked. The normal trivialities of small talk were missing.

From Warrnambool Sam and I went to Hamilton to see my cousin. She had been my strongest support when I was writing from America and had claimed to understand and support me in every way. When I arrived we chatted and she told me that Mandy had called from Warrnambool to discuss her discomfort with having me in the house. I subsequently found that similar calls were being placed ahead of me wherever I went. My aunt had also called Mandy after we had left Melbourne, but before we arrived in Warrnambool.

The trip to see my cousin was a disaster. She had not been well for some years, and had not recovered as well as she had suggested in our letters to each other. She was still quite ill. When Sam and I arrived it was evident that she was in total shock at having me as a guest. The morning degenerated to the point where she finally came out and asked that question: "If you don't want to make love to a man why did you go to all the trouble of having a sex change operation? If you want to live with and have sex with a woman why didn't you stay a man?"

There were so many misunderstandings in her questions, so many errors that I didn't even know where to start to answer her. Here was someone who was well-educated, had experienced much in her young life, and yet she had not comprehended any-thing that I had been telling her through those months of letter writing. We went to the depths of our problems in those letters, how no one in the family wanted to know about what we were going through, how much help it was just having one person in the family in whom we could confide.

I had explained carefully to her that transgenderism was a matter of gender, not sexuality. I had explained how gender was a core feeling, how it went to the very heart of who I was. I explained that it was different from my sexual feelings, my choice between male and female for a sexual partner. I had explained that transgendered people could be gay or straight, just like anyone else.

She had written back and said that she understood, and that she had no problem with me being both transgendered and les-bian. And yet here we were, sitting three feet from each other, and she could still ask the question.

I sat back in my chair, cradled the warm tea cup in my hands and squinted out into the harsh sunlight. Galahs were calling from the tops of the cypress trees that broke the strong west wind before it reached the house. A few sheep stood forlornly in the paddock of dry, brown grass, all the feed that was left after a long hot summer.

I changed the subject and asked how the season had been. Had the wool prices gotten better? Had they considered chang-ing to meat-lamb breeding? I wanted to get back to the safe, triv-ial chatter that went with morning tea on a country verandah, away from sexuality and all those other psychological giants that we were both struggling with. I knew that I would have to do a lot of educating about transgenderism if I ever wanted my fami-ly and friends to know who I was and why I had to change.

Chapter Seventeen

When I got back to Melbourne I thought I should make some contacts so I called a local transgendered group and arranged to go to their monthly meeting. It was a good night and again I was being watched over. They had a guest speaker by the name of Sue and after the talk we got together and found that we got on quite well. I gave her my number and we arranged to meet the next day for lunch. The lunch was very pleasant and I told her that I would write from America when I got back.

I thought the trip was going reasonably well as far as meeting family was concerned, and Sam and I were enjoying our holiday together. Then, a day or two after returning from Hamilton, I put my back out and was immobilized for four days. It had happened before but not for two years. I had been standing in the bathroom drying myself when I felt a click and a jab of pain. My father took me to the chiropractor, but afterwards Sam still had to help me dress each morning. It was obviously hard for my father to have me around the house so much.

As soon as I could move with only minimal pain, Sam and I rented a car and drove the three hundred and fifty miles to Wonboyn on the far south coast of New South Wales. We had a wonderful time and stayed there, away from the family, fishing and exploring until three days before we were to return to America.

I showed Sam all the places I had loved so much. The long river that ended in a series of shallow rock pools overhung by trees. The estuary with its black cormorants and white pelicans.

The ocean beach that was so secluded that you could walk naked along the sand and watch dolphins and sharks suspended in the face of the waves that broke along the beach. We caught fish and walked through the bush, enjoying the opportunity to be completely alone together.

When we got back to Melbourne we said our farewells and my father drove us to the airport. An hour later we were in Sydney waiting for the next flight. Sam and I wandered around the airport and finally sat down together at a quiet end of the lounge where we looked out the windows and read. There were some trees in the distance and sea gulls wheeled over the water of the wetland around the airport. A couple of magpies flew past. All of a sudden I started to cry. Unstoppable tears streamed down my face. I realized that my heart was breaking, and that leaving Australia to return to America was the silliest thing I had ever done in my life. It was time to return home for good.

I have no idea what triggered my feelings as I sat looking out the window, but I knew that when I got back to America I had to say good-bye, pack my belongings, and return to Australia as fast as I could.

After we got back and settled down from the trip Laurie told me that she was moving to Rhode Island to live with her partner Brian. With Sam and Laurie leaving Vermont I felt that my decision to return to Australia was confirmed for me, and I started making plans.

Initially I had planned to leave as soon after Christmas as possible. I wanted a discount fare, which meant waiting until March, so I set that as the time. Within a week I decided there was no point staying past Christmas. I would leave as soon as Sam and Laurie moved to Rhode Island, in January.

The more I thought about it the more I realized that I was just procrastinating, that I wanted to leave as soon as possible. I called the travel agent again and found that the last day of off-peak travel for 1993 was November 30, so I booked a seat for that day.

Having finally set the date I no longer concerned myself with finding a job. I did part-time work just to keep up some sort of cash flow. I also had a few personal commitments and loose ends to finalize. The main one was to complete my poetry course with Pam. I wrote and rewrote poems until I had a manuscript of sixty-four poems and bound them as a book. I made fifteen copies and handed them out to those friends who had supported me over the eight years I had lived in Vermont.

As the departure date drew closer, fear and depression started to rise up again. I realized I was moving away from all my support networks and into a place where I knew I was not going to be welcome. I was also at a point in my life when I was waiting for something to happen.

Fall was coming and the days were getting shorter. Frost was forming on the windscreens and windows. I was going away. Away where? I wondered. Was I running away from life? Was living in Vermont without Sam and Laurie too threatening for me? Did I need to escape and start again with new friends and contacts? But this rush to Australia had started before I had found out that they were leaving.

Was I being silly trying to find answers for all these questions? I did not know. Was I going too far inside my head? Did I need to stop digging through the rubble, making my mind bleed like fingers torn by broken masonry? Was it all a need to turn my back on the past and start anew?

I looked at what I had done, what I had achieved in those seven short years in America. I recalled the progress I had made. In seven years and seven months I had built a whole new life. It was time to stop thinking and worrying. I had made my decision and it was time to start acting again.

I did some research on sending things back to Australia and found that the cheapest way was to mail them, so I saw Ferne at the Strafford post office and bought boxes and tape. Many large items such as furniture and my car I sold or gave away. Some heavy things like records I stored with Laurie's parents on the off chance that I would find the money some day to send for them. Everything else of importance I packed and mailed. I ended up sending thirty-four boxes, sixteen of which were full of books. A couple contained household items like dishes and vases, the rest contained clothes.

The only large item I sent back was a print Laurie and I had bought in Connecticut, many years before when we lived there. It was of an otter in a lake, with an island covered in evergreens in the background, a picture that always transports me back to northern New England.

Thanksgiving was my last time with all the family. Laurie and Sam came up from Rhode Island and we had a few days together. I was looking forward to it but at the same time I knew it would be hard to say my farewells. I was both excited and depressed once more.

News from Australia added to my depression. I had known I would not be particularly welcome on my return but it was worse than I had thought. My father wrote to say that he did not want me to stay with him, even for one night. In the past such a rejection would have devastated me, now I was seeing his rejection as a possible blessing. I was being forced to become more independent.

I called Sue, the friend I had made in Australia the previous June, and asked if she had a spare bed I could use for a few nights. She said I was welcome to the couch in her living room until I found somewhere else to stay. She said she could also collect me from the airport, thereby relieving my family of the responsibility and inconvenience. I was on my way and, not only that, I was assured of a friendly welcome when I arrived, even if it wasn't from my family.

It was now only six days before my departure. I discarded belongings so fast I felt like a parched traveler running toward an oasis, running faster and faster as I neared the water.

At first I thought I wanted to take as much memorabilia as possible back with me. As I looked at things, I saw that I really didn't need them. They were just not important to me any more.

I did wonder, though, if when I got back I could keep my

material possessions simple. Could I live in a flat with a bed, a few pieces of furniture, a comfortable reading chair and maybe a couch? Could I change my lifestyle to a point verging on Bohemian? I thought it might be fun to try. I wanted to pare my belongings down to the point where I was free to move on a whim. I wanted to become a free, or at least liberated, spirit. I imagined living in a flat with lots of prints, books, CDs, a VCR, a futon and one chair. I wanted a life of plays, movies, book groups, bird watching and weekends of writing at Wonboyn.

As I said my goodbyes to friends, one of them, Ina, told me about the Sixth International Feminist Book Fair that would be happening in Melbourne after I returned. It seemed too good to be true. It was an opportunity to work, even as a volunteer, at an event that I really wanted to be a part of.

On my last morning in Vermont I left a copy of my poems on Deb's bed with a note of thanks and then drove around seeing Nora, Pat, Danette and some of my other friends. We had a last hug and promised to keep in touch.

I arrived at Laurie's parents' house, put my suitcase in their car and we left for Boston. At the airport I said farewell to them, and to Sam and Laurie who had driven up from Rhode Island, and boarded the plane for Melbourne.

On November 30 I crossed the international date line and landed in Australia on December 2.

Chapter Eighteen

Sue lived in Fitzroy, an eclectic Melbourne suburb of cafes, bookstores, and row houses. After she collected me from the airport we went back to her house and I had a short rest and a shower before she rushed me off to a night at the theater. I had rashly agreed to go to some women's performances. For the first half of the performance I was fine but after intermission the thirty-four hour flight started to catch up with me. I nodded through the second half of the performance. It would not have been so bad except that it was a one woman show, a very small audience, and we had front row seats. I tried pinching my arm, breathing deeply, and doing eye exercises, but nothing helped. My head slowly lowered again and again until I snapped back to semi-consciousness. By the time we got home I was so tired I could hardly think.

The next morning I woke early and was once more confronted by my early morning nemesis: depression. It cast a shadow over my strength and resolve and made me wonder what I was doing back in Australia. Like some dark current of smoke, it drew me inexorably into fear and loneliness.

As I lay on the couch in Sue's living room, my depression told me I was crazy. It pointed out that I was alone and unemployed in a big city, that I didn't have a degree in anything, that the country had thirteen percent unemployment and that I hadn't had a real job for ten months.

A fog of doubt swirled around me and I longed for the security of Sharon, Vermont, where I had had a safety net: Betty, Deb,

Nora, and many others. In Australia I had nothing.

I sat up and realized that it was my first morning in Australia and I was not on the street but in a warm bed. The city was full of possibilities and I was no worse off than I had been twenty-four hours before. I knew that if I continued step by step, all would be well. If I gave myself a month or two I could develop a firm new foundation.

I settled back into life in Melbourne faster than I had expected. Within a week I was asked if I wanted to volunteer at a new gay and lesbian radio station. They needed someone to answer the phones for one of the women's programs. It sounded like fun. When I arrived one of the two women I was to be helping said, "Come in here and sit down. We need someone to read announcements."

I had never been on any sort of radio program. I had done no more public speaking than I had needed for my courses at college, but I thought "Why not?" and followed them into the studio and went on air.

My first real job was working for the Book Fair as its publicity and promotion officer. It was a wonderful job that gave me an opportunity to meet and work with some talented and creative people. The hours were long, often sixteen or seventeen a day, seven days a week, but the result was a major success. We had over two hundred readers and presenters from more than thirty countries. The five day event attracted over twenty thousand visitors. The majority of the feedback we received afterwards was so supportive that it made all the effort well worthwhile.

For me the stress was incredible. I not only had to produce all the publicity and arrange interviews for the invited authors, I felt obliged to keep my past a secret. This was not because I was ashamed of who I was. If I had been confronted I would not have denied it, but I did not want anything to detract from the aim and purpose of the event, which was to provide a forum for women's writing from around the world. By the end of the event I was exhausted and did something I had never done before. I had a total sobbing, crying, screaming, wall kicking, door slamming burn-out fit.

One person I had met during the fair was Michelle. We had worked together and gotten to know each other as friends. During the fair we talked of sharing a house together to try and cut some of our costs. At the time we were both living alone.

After the Book Fair, things calmed down and I broached the subject with her again. We arranged to go to a cafe and discuss it. I knew by then that for me to have a close friendship I needed to be open about my past. I planned to tell Michelle everything before she made a final decision about sharing a house with me. Sitting in the cafe after our meal I said, "Michelle, if we are sharing a house together there is something that you need to know."

She said, "I think I know what you're going to tell me and don't worry it's okay." One of the Book Fair volunteers had outed me to many of the workers.

After moving in together we were both surprised by the growth of feelings between us. Before long our friendship developed into a relationship and I realized how good life can be. We both had the same interest in writing and travel so my life had almost gone in a full circle. Where I once did these things as John now I started to do them again as Jen.

We went back to the Hattah lakes/Kulkyne area in northeast Victoria to walk in the desert and watch parrots. We went down to Wonboyn and ate oysters fresh from the rocks, washed down with cold white wine. We spent weekends at Wonthaggi and Warratah Bay walking the beaches collecting sea shells and marveling at the beauty of the sea. We stayed with friends in the country, feeding the chooks and throwing hay to the cattle from the back of a tractor.

While I did all the things I loved so much, with someone I loved, I had the same emotional feelings as I used to have. I was surrounded by nature and beauty, thrilled by the sight of birds and plants, but now I had a spirit that was not clouded by the guilt of lying to my partner and wondering how much longer it would go on before I was discovered as a fraud and abandoned as a pervert. I no longer had a dark cloud over me and I allowed myself to express all my emotions as they came to me. I had reached the point where I was free to perform the 'manly' chores of fixing engines, and heaving hay bales. I could also revel in the freedom of the more feminine joys like smoothing on a scented skin-care creme at the end of the day.

After all the acrimony in his earlier letters I realized it was my father who ultimately put in the most effort to accept me. I knew it was very hard for him to have his only son change to live out her life openly as a woman. My feelings toward him mellowed as I came to accept that he was from a generation that was very different from mine: sex was never discussed and things like homosexuality and transsexuality only happened to other people's families, never to one's own.

I persevered against his obvious discomfort during our visits and eventually when I went to see him we could sit and talk much as we had in the past. The content of our conversations was never challenging and on many subjects, like politics, where our views differed greatly, I never pushed him. We were never at any time of my life particularly close, but we were friends, and I would like to think that he was slowly coming to accept me for who I was. Sadly, he died on the September 30, 1995, after a short illness. Now we will never have the chance to become close.

At his funeral I realized just how much my being transgendered had isolated me from some old friends and contacts. Few of my father's friends came over to speak with me. They had not seen me in over eight years and they were obviously uncomfortable with my presence and kept a discrete distance.

One old school friend of mine moved to the periphery of the group and left without a word. Others grouped together in their dark business suits, doing their best to avoid eye contact with me. I became more and more rigid. I wanted to appear relaxed and welcoming but I doubt that my body language was conveying that message.

There was a cold wind on that overcast day and Michelle and

I stood together at the curb outside the chapel with one or two of the mourners. Everyone else congregated around my sisters or chatted among themselves. I approached a few but the conversations were brief and strained. When the doors opened and we moved inside, the family pew at the front filled with extended family. Michelle and I were left to sit across the aisle on the front pew that was empty. Even though there were not enough seats for everyone in the chapel only two other people sat in our pew. I overheard someone say from across the aisle, "Look, no one wants to sit with them."

An old friend of my father's gave the eulogy. "Edwin was a facilitator for the family. He made things happen but he never directly instigated them," he said.

This was very accurate. It was my father who brought my mother's numerous ideas to fruition. After my mother died, it was his presence in many situations that caused members of the family to contact each other.

After the service I hoped that some of my old friends would speak to me. One cousin whom I had not seen since I was about fifteen did, providing wonderful support by standing with us, telling stories and releasing some of the tension. His support was so welcome and refreshing that it made it possible for both Michelle and me to relax a little. I laughed at some of his comments and although some people may have seen our laughter as irreverent, it was the thing that allowed me to get through the day.

We returned to my aunt's house for the wake and a tolerant few spoke to Michelle and me. Others kept the length of the room between us. I stayed for an hour but soon the continual misuse of my old name and the male pronoun started to sadden both of us.

My immediate family still does not fully accept my change. Some, like my aunt and her daughter, have been very friendly and our relationship is much as it ever was. They have been very supportive and loving. My sister Mandy has changed over the years, and we have drifted apart. We are now on speaking terms but not much more than that. As I have said, I truly regret this because I used to think we were close. I rarely see my youngest sister, Gina. Since she is so much younger, and I have been away for much of her life, it would take tremendous time and effort to develop a relationship with her.

My sisters and I have all grown and changed and our formerly common links and interests are no longer in place. Until both sides wish to reestablish them, it will not happen. Despite what a lot of people think, I don't believe that blood is thicker than water.

Conclusion

Now I am living on the other side of the world from my little one-room school house. No longer do I look out on a sylvan scene of Vermont beauty, but on to a flowering Australian bottle-brush tree, crimson-red, in a sunny backyard in Melbourne. The sounds of cows and sheep have been replaced by the rattle of trams and trucks in nearby St. Georges Road and the smell of pine trees by the smell of diesel fumes and wet bitumen. It is the antithesis of where I started writing this book, yet I could not be more content.

Perhaps the only real lifestyle changes I have found since I returned from America are the need to conform to some of the traditional social customs of Australia, and knowing the fear that all women have of living in a city. I can no longer go into a public bar of a country hotel (or any hotel public bar for that matter) and lean against the bar and listen to the chat and stories of the locals. I have learned that men are now a danger to me. While driving home I was followed by a man in a car who eventually stopped beside mine and propositioned me. I have had the same thing happen while walking down the street in the middle of the day. I have suffered while some pervert stalked Michelle and me, despite the fact that we had a restraining order taken out against him. None of these things ever happened to me while I was living as a man. They are dangers almost unique to women and I now have to seriously consider where I go and when. I have to look down a footpath and plan ahead in case someone steps from a driveway, or from behind a bush. I have to cross the road and avoid the group of men loitering outside the hotel door, and I have to be aware of who is following down the path behind me as I take my daily walk in the park—things that very few men have to worry about. These risks are all part and parcel of my choice to come out and live the rest of my life openly as a woman, but I would never go back. I can still say that there has not been one day, even one moment, that I have regretted my decision and, if given the chance to do it all over, the only thing I would do differently would be to have started many years earlier.

There are emotional risks in telling this story. As a transgendered lesbian I take a double risk, coming out both in society in general, as well as in my own community of friends. This risk exists because current feelings in both the heterosexual and gay communities are divided over the place and role of people who are born transgendered, both those who are male-to-female and those who are female-to-male.

As an example, two women with whom I worked at the Book Fair were so shocked when they learned of my background that they started a rumor among my friends and acquaintances that I was an abusive partner and was violent toward Michelle. Their purpose was to put pressure on people to see that my relationship with Michelle was ended. Within our immediate friends the ploy did not work but I am left to wonder how many people within the wider community believed the stories.

People are taught to fear those who are different from what society currently defines as 'normal,' be it physically, mentally, sexually, or racially. If we could only accept each other's individuality as special and enriching for the whole, much of the suffering could be avoided and many of the cosmetic changes we make to our bodies to gain acceptance would not be necessary. And the risks to my private life and to those who are close to me would not exist.

When, after many years of living in a manner that allowed me to be accepted by society as a well-adjusted male heterosexual, I finally took the step to change my outward appearance to female and began living as I had cognitively always known I should—as a woman—it was extremely hard. In order to maintain my mask of masculinity I had hidden my desires so well that very few people knew what I was going through. My changing was made even harder by the fact that, having made the decision, there were few role models for me to follow.

This lack of role models stems from a variety of reasons. First, in a patriarchal system, transgenderism is often seen by those who set the standards, the men, as the ultimate defection. It is seen as either wantonly giving up the superiority of being male, or conversely in the case of female-to-male transition, assuming a position to which, by birth, a person is not entitled.

Second, most men feel a severe physical threat at the suggestion of having a penis removed, even when it is not their own. Just the thought can be such an affront to their psyche they tend to react violently in self-righteous protection against anyone who removes a penis.

Third, transgendered people compose a very small section of the possible variations in the broad spectrum of gender and sexual variations that make up the human species. It is believed that only one person in every eighty to one hundred thousand is transgendered. Only an estimated twenty to forty percent of that very small number are homosexual. Worldwide there are many thousands, but as a percentage of the total, still not many.

Finally, the majority of this very small number of people have only one desire after changing from one outward gender role to another, and that is to become invisible. After living a life of persecution, both mental and physical, their only desire is to blend into their chosen gender and become what is often so tritely called 'normal people.'

One role model that I could have followed was that of the show-girl and dancer, but that was not me. What I wanted was to live as a professional woman with a career that was productive and beneficial to other people. The majority of transgendered people who have gone this route became invisible and therefore unavailable for me to emulate. For the sake of others following I will remain one of the small group that is visible.

Medical knowledge has advanced to where it has accepted that not everything can be known about a person just by merely looking at physical attributes. It is time for the medical profession to universally accept this and relinquish their dogma that a person's gender is determined by genitalia. We are all much more than just a penis or a vagina. It is, I grant, a convenient first indication of a person's gender that is normally fairly accurate, but if an intelligent individual comes to the realization that he or she has been wrongly diagnosed at birth, then I believe it is that person's right to change, and have society accept their decision to change.

I am transgendered, as are thousands of others, and there is nothing I can do about it. People who are born transgendered have very limited avenues available to them and sooner or later they need to select one. We need to find a lifestyle that allows us to express our preferred gender. It is only recently that enough has been published that would allow people to make an educated decision. There is not enough information available yet for parents to easily help a child who believes he or she may be transgendered. One thing that I am sure of is that Dr. Shaefer was correct: the only option not available is to do nothing. There is no cure.

I have made my choices in life and I am now living as an openly lesbian woman in a relationship. I am still not yet, and may never be, totally open about my gender dysphoria. In our society, even within the lesbian and gay communities, equal rights do not extend to everyone.

I said in my introduction that society sees me as a woman; it does not, in the majority of places in the world, however, see me as legally female. My birth certificate still says I am male and I cannot legally marry a man. In a court of law I can still be convicted and sent to a men's prison. In the case of workplace discrimination I can still be dismissed from a job purely because I am transgendered, and I have no recourse in law.

In some sections of the lesbian community the animosity against patriarchy is so intense that anyone associated with it, in any way, is suspect. The feeling is that transgendered people are insidious interlopers who are infiltrating the lesbian community and thereby maintaining a degree of patriarchal hold over it. I find this perspective sad. I am not trying to invade any group, I am trying to be accepted for who I am, and that is not a man.

Prior to my change I did not see myself as taking a stereotypical male sexual role, either in the bedroom or in society. I lived as a person who did what was loving and required to help support a family. Because of my background I went to work each day and followed the male role but it was not because I wanted to, it was because of societal and peer pressure.

Before my change, I was basically asexual. During those rare times we did have sex I felt trapped by Laurie's expectations and preferences, and my upbringing, to behave like a man—'dominant' (but not violent or aggressive). I always fantasized that I had a vagina, not a penis.

My desires, now that I know the joys of sex, are as varied and transitory as those of any other person. Sex roles and sexual activities are not something linked to being transgendered any more than being gay or heterosexual is. Expressions of top/bottom, femme/butch behavior are fluid within my current relationship and change with my mood and that of my partner, insofar as any of our behavior can be defined in such terms.

We do not identify with butch/femme roles per se, but I do believe that what is done lovingly and without injury or threat is acceptable behavior. It is also the business of those involved and should not have to be justified or defended in public.

On the first page of the introduction I quoted my cousin as saying, "If you don't want to make love to a man why did you go to all the trouble of having a sex change operation?" I now know that the necessity to ask this question comes not only from society's ignorance of what it is to be a transgendered lesbian, but also from an ignorance of what it is to be a lesbian. Many people have no idea of the sexual pleasures of a lesbian lifestyle. Satisfying sex, to them, requires the presence of a penis, and penetration. The multiplicity of pleasures possible without this appendage does not enter their imagination. This is not a book in which I want to enter into that discussion, but suffice it to say, this lack of knowledge adds to misunderstanding.

I am also finding that, as I talk to more heterosexual people, they expect that all transgendered people remain heterosexual after the change. They expect me to want a male sexual partner, not a female one. When I tell them I am a lesbian, as well as being transgendered, they go through a second period of shock. My cousin's opinion was just the expression of a common belief held by a majority of society.

Finally, now that I have reached the point in my life where I have finished making the radical changes to my body that allow me to live in our society as a woman, I want to emphasize that I regret very little of my early years and feel that they were productive and fulfilling. The part of me that was John I do not want to forget or deny. I want to continue my life, living by all my life experiences. The moral education given to me during my early years is very important, and the fact that it was given to John does not lessen its quality in any way. It has given me the strength to confront and solve my gender dysphoria, and resume a productive life.

Part of this new productive life is all my new friends, male and female, gay and straight. They are my workmates, teachers and fellow students. They are the people I have met through my writing and they are the people from my past who have come to know me as I always wanted them to.

As I finish this book I hope that all who read it will gain some understanding of what it means to be transgendered. It is not an easy life, but no life is. With tolerance and understanding it is possible to change one's birth-allocated gender and enjoy life to its full. Not once, even on the worst day in the last five years have I thought that what I was doing was a mistake. The only thing I completely failed at in my life was trying to be someone I never was—a man.